Being a Writer™

Funding for Developmental Studies Center has been generously provided by:

The Annenberg Foundation, Inc.

The Atlantic Philanthropies (USA) Inc.

The Robert Bowne Foundation, Inc.

The Annie E. Casey Foundation

Center for Substance Abuse Prevention:
  Substance Abuse and Mental Health Services Agency,
  U.S. Department of Health and Human Services

The Danforth Foundation

The DuBarry Foundation

The Ford Foundation

William T. Grant Foundation

Evelyn and Walter Haas, Jr. Fund

Walter and Elise Haas Fund

J. David and Pamela Hakman Family Foundation

Hasbro Children's Foundation

Charles Hayden Foundation

The William Randolph Hearst Foundation

Clarence E. Heller Charitable Foundation

The William and Flora Hewlett Foundation

The James Irvine Foundation

The Robert Wood Johnson Foundation

Walter S. Johnson Foundation

Ewing Marion Kauffman Foundation

W.K. Kellogg Foundation

John S. and James L. Knight Foundation

Lilly Endowment, Inc.

The MBK Foundation

Mr. and Mrs. Sanford N. McDonnell

The John D. and Catherine T. MacArthur Foundation

A.L. Mailman Family Foundation, Inc.

Charles Stewart Mott Foundation

National Institute on Drug Abuse (NIDA),
  National Institutes of Health

National Science Foundation

Nippon Life Insurance Foundation

Karen and Christopher Payne Foundation

The Pew Charitable Trusts

The Pinkerton Foundation

The Rockefeller Foundation

Louise and Claude Rosenberg, Jr. Family Foundation

The San Francisco Foundation

Shinnyo-En Foundation

Silver Giving Foundation

The Spencer Foundation

Spunk Fund, Inc.

Stuart Foundation

The Stupski Family Foundation

The Sulzberger Foundation, Inc.

Surdna Foundation, Inc.

John Templeton Foundation

U.S. Department of Education

Wallace-Reader's Digest Funds

Wells Fargo Bank

Grade K

VOLUME **2**
TEACHER'S MANUAL

Being a Writer™

DEVELOPMENTAL STUDIES CENTER™

Copyright © 2007 Developmental Studies Center

All rights reserved. Except where otherwise noted, no part of this publication may be reproduced in whole or in part, or stored in a retrieval system, or transmitted in any form or by any means, electronic, mechanical, photocopying, recording, or otherwise, without the written permission of the publisher. For information regarding permissions, write to the Editorial Department at Developmental Studies Center.

Permission is granted to reproduce the blackline masters in this volume for classroom use only.

Being a Writer is a trademark of Developmental Studies Center.

Developmental Studies Center wishes to thank the following authors, agents, and publishers for their permission to reprint materials included in this program. Many people went out of their way to help us secure these rights and we are very grateful for their support. Every effort has been made to trace the ownership of copyrighted material and to make full acknowledgment of its use. If errors or omissions have occurred, they will be corrected in subsequent editions, provided that notification has been submitted in writing to the publisher.

"Wide Awake" from *Wide Awake and Other Poems* by Myra Cohn Livingston. Copyright © 1959, 1987 Myra Cohn Livingston. Used by permission of Marian Reiner. "Shore" by Mary Britton Miller appears in *Read-Aloud Rhymes for the Very Young*, copyright © 1986, edited by Jack Prelutsky and published by Random House Children's Books.

A special thanks to Donald Murray (who passed away December 30, 2006) for the wonderful assortment of author quotations that he gathered in his book *shoptalk: learning to write with writers*, published by Boynton/Cook Publishers in 1990.

Developmental Studies Center
2000 Embarcadero, Suite 305
Oakland, CA 94606-5300
(800) 666-7270, fax: (510) 464-3670
www.devstu.org

ISBN-13: 978-1-59892-289-9
ISBN-10: 1-59892-289-0

Printed in the United States of America

1 2 3 4 5 6 7 8 9 10 MLY 11 10 09 08 07

TABLE OF CONTENTS

Unit 3 Telling More 195
    Week 1 199
    Week 2 213
    Week 3 228
    Week 4 246

Unit 4 Just the Facts 261
    Week 1 264
    Week 2 280
    Week 3 296

Unit 5 Exploring Words Through Poetry 311
    Week 1 314
    Week 2 330
    Week 3 350

Unit 6 Revisiting the Writing Community 367
    Week 1 369

Skill Development Chart 384

Bibliography 385

Blackline Master 389

Unit 3

Telling More

Unit 3

Telling More

During this four-week unit, the students explore telling more in their stories by adding to their illustrations and writing. Before they write, they think and talk about what they want to say, and they revisit their drawings and think about what they can add to them; then they use their drawings to help them tell more in their writing. They write shared stories, choose topics for their own stories, and share their writing from the Author's Chair. They continue to approximate spelling and use a word wall to spell high-frequency sight words. Socially, they develop the skills of listening to their partner carefully and sharing their partner's thinking and writing with the class. They also learn the prompts "I found out" and "I want to know" to help them express interest in one another's writing.

UNIT OVERVIEW

WEEK	DAY 1	DAY 2	DAY 3
1	**Choosing Topics and Writing Stories** **Focus:** • Contributing to a shared story • Visualizing and writing about topics they choose	**Rereading and Telling More** **Focus:** • Rereading and adding to stories • Approximating spelling and using the word wall • Capitalizing and punctuating sentences	**Sharing as a Community** **Focus:** • Learning the prompt "I found out" • Writing and drawing freely
2	**Choosing Topics and Writing Stories** **Focus:** • Contributing to a shared story • Visualizing and writing about topics they choose • Capitalizing and punctuating sentences	**Rereading and Telling More** **Focus:** • Rereading and adding to stories • Approximating spelling and using the word wall	**Sharing as a Community** **Focus:** • Learning the prompt "I want to know" • Writing and drawing freely
3	**Writing Stories:** *Cookie's Week* **Focus:** • Exploring how a professional author tells more • Writing about weekly activities	**Rereading and Telling More** **Focus:** • Rereading and adding to stories • Approximating spelling and using the word wall	**Author's Chair Sharing** **Focus:** • Sharing stories from the Author's Chair • Practicing the prompts "I found out" and "I want to know" • Writing and drawing freely
4	**Writing Stories:** *When Sophie Gets Angry— Really, Really Angry…* **Focus:** • Exploring how a professional author tells more • Writing about when they get "really, really angry"	**Rereading and Telling More** **Focus:** • Rereading and adding to stories • Approximating spelling and using the word wall	**Author's Chair Sharing** **Focus:** • Sharing stories from the Author's Chair • Using the prompts "I found out" and "I want to know" • Writing and drawing freely

Week 1 Overview

UNIT 3: TELLING MORE

Writing Focus

- Students contribute to shared stories and write their own.
- Students select their own topics for writing.
- Students visualize to get story ideas.
- Students reread their stories and tell more.
- Students approximate spelling and use the word wall.
- Students explore capitalizing the first letters of sentences and using periods at the ends.

Social Focus

- Students listen respectfully to the thinking of others and share their own.
- Students express interest in and appreciation for one another's writing.
- Students act in fair and caring ways.

DO AHEAD

- Prior to Day 1, decide how you will randomly assign partners to work together during this unit. See the front matter in volume 1 for suggestions about assigning partners randomly (page xiii) and for considerations for pairing English Language Learners (page xxvi).
- Prior to Day 1, review the writing ideas charts from Unit 2 and choose a topic from one of the charts to write about in a shared story (see the diagram on page 202 for an example).
- Prior to Day 1, prepare a sheet of chart paper so it looks like an enlarged version of the writing/drawing paper the students will use.

TEACHER AS WRITER

"To swim well, we must let ourselves be enveloped by the water, sink into it, become a part of it. To write well, we must similarly let ourselves be enveloped by the language, sink into it, become a part of it."
— Thomas Szasz

This week, review the lists you wrote in Units 1 and 2 and pick one topic that intrigues you. Jot down a few broad ideas about the topic, asking yourself:

- What makes this topic important?
- What are two very significant things about this topic?

Start with one of your ideas and write freely about the topic, incorporating new ideas as they come to you. Try to "sink into" the topic and fill several sheets if you can.

Kindergarten | 199

Unit 3 ▶ Week 1

Day 1

Choosing Topics and Writing Stories

Materials
- Writing ideas charts from Unit 2
- Chart paper (see "Do Ahead" on page 199) and a marker

In this lesson, the students:
- Work with a new partner
- Contribute to a shared story
- Visualize and write about topics that interest them
- Approximate spelling and use the word wall
- Treat one another as friends

About Telling More

Young writers typically know more about a topic than they write, as their oral retellings of their stories show. In this unit, the students focus on telling more about their topic by adding details to their drawing and writing. They learn and practice strategies for telling more both *before* and *after* they write. Before they write, they visualize, think, and talk about the information they might include in their story. After they write, they reread their story by looking at their drawings and words and think about what more they can tell. They also hear and discuss books that exemplify telling more.

GETTING READY TO WRITE

1 Pair Students and Discuss Working Together

Randomly assign partners and make sure they know each other's names (see "Do Ahead" on page 199). Gather the class with partners sitting together, facing you. Explain during the next few weeks they will work with a new partner to talk about and share their writing. Ask and briefly discuss:

Q *What will you do to be a good friend to your partner today?*

Q *Why is it important that you treat your partner as a friend?*

Making Meaning® Teacher
You can either have the students work with their *Making Meaning* partner or assign a different partner for the writing lessons.

 **ELL Note**

You might provide the prompt "I will be a good friend by" to your English Language Learners to help them verbalize their answers to these questions.

Unit 3 ▸ Week 1 ▸ Day 1

Students might say:

"I will talk to my partner in a nice voice."

"I will be a good friend to my partner by helping her if she needs help."

"It's important to be a friend to your partner so you can both learn."

"If both partners treat each other as friends, they'll both feel good in school."

Encourage the students to keep their ideas in mind as they work with their new partner today.

Think About and Write a Shared Story

Remind the students that over the past several weeks they heard and wrote many stories and made many lists of writing ideas. Explain that during the next few weeks they will think about how they can tell more in their stories by adding to their drawings and words.

Explain that the students will practice telling more by writing a story together. Ask the students to watch as you model using the writing ideas charts from Unit 2 to choose an idea for the story. Briefly review the charts and choose an idea that will engage the students. Think aloud about the story; then write the first sentence and draw a simple picture to start the story.

As you write, point out that you are starting your sentence with a capital letter and you are ending it with a period. Also continue to refer to the word wall and to approximate the spelling of unfamiliar words, as you did in Unit 2.

Telling More

FACILITATION TIP

During this unit, we invite you to practice **asking facilitative questions** during class discussions to help the students respond directly to one another, not just to you. After a student comments, ask the class questions such as:

Q *Do you agree or disagree with [Deborah]? Why?*

Q *What can you add to what [Deborah] said?*

Teacher Note

You might say, "Let's look through our ideas charts to get an idea for our story. One idea we have on our 'Interesting Things' chart is the duck we saw in the pond. Let's write our story about him. I'm going to start our story by writing, *We saw a duck.* Next I'll draw the duck."

Teacher Note

Continue to look for opportunities to sound out words and approximate spelling using the procedure you used in Unit 2, Week 7, Day 2 (page 149). For example:

Q *[Duck] starts with the [/d/] sound. What letter is that?*

Q *What sound do you hear next in the word [d-u-ck]? What letter(s) can make that sound?*

Q *What's the [next/last] sound? What letter(s) can make that sound?*

Always model correct spelling unless you are deliberately modeling an approximate spelling.

Kindergarten

Telling More Unit 3 ▶ Week 1 ▶ Day 1

> _____We saw a duck._____
> _____
> _____

Reread the story and explain that you would like the students' help to tell more in the story. Have the students close their eyes and make pictures in their minds as you ask questions like the ones that follow, one at a time. Pause between each question to give the students time to think.

Q *Where did we see the [duck]?*

Q *What did the [duck] look like?*

Q *What did we see or hear around us?*

Q *What was the [duck] doing?*

Have the students open their eyes. Use "Think, Pair, Share" to have the students first think about and then discuss:

 **Q** *What can we add to our picture to tell more about our story?* [pause] *Turn to your partner.*

Signal for the students' attention and have a few volunteers share their thinking with the class.

Teacher Note

If the students have difficulty suggesting additional ideas, think aloud and model adding to your illustration. ▶

202 | Being a Writer™

Students might say:

"The duck should be by a pond."

"We should color the duck."

"We could add the sun in the sky."

"We could put grass around the pond."

"There were trees around the pond, too."

Use the students' suggestions to add details to the picture. Retell the story by reading the words and telling about the details in the picture. Point out how adding to the picture tells more about the story and makes it more interesting. Explain that today the students will have a chance to write their own stories and tell more by adding to their pictures.

Visualize and Share Story Ideas

Explain that the students may write a story about anything they choose today. Review the writing ideas charts from Unit 2 and tell them that they may write a story about one of the charted topics, if they wish. Give them a few moments to decide on a topic to write about.

Have the students close their eyes and make a picture in their mind as you ask the following questions, one at a time. Pause between each question to give the students time to think.

Q *What are you going to write about today?*

Q *What's happening in your story?*

Q *Where is your story happening?*

Q *Who is in your story?*

Have the students open their eyes. Use "Think, Pair, Share" to have partners first think about and then discuss:

Q *What did you picture in your mind to write about today?* [pause] *Turn to your partner.*

Signal for the students' attention and have a few volunteers share their ideas with the class.

> **Students might say:**
>
> "I went to the park with my dad. I'm going to draw my dad and me next to a slide."
>
> "My grandma came to visit us. I'll draw her and my house."
>
> "My story is about my dog. I'm going to draw him and write *I have a dog*."

Encourage the students to use the ideas they shared with their partner in their stories today.

WRITING TIME

4 Write and Draw Stories

Have the students return to their seats and distribute the writing/drawing paper. Encourage them to sound out words and use the word wall to help them with their spelling. When they have settled into their writing, walk around and observe.

After 10–15 minutes, signal for the students' attention. Have the students take a moment to reread their story and look at their illustration; then ask:

Q *What can you add to your picture to tell more in your story?* [pause] *Turn to your partner.*

After a few moments, signal for the students' attention. Without discussing the question as a class, have the students resume their independent work. Encourage them to add to their pictures to tell more.

Signal to let the students know when writing time is over. Ask and briefly discuss:

Q *What did you add to your drawing after you talked to your partner?*

Collect the students' stories and tell the students that they will add more to their stories tomorrow.

REFLECTING

 Reflect on Working with a New Partner

Ask and briefly discuss:

Q *What did you do to treat your partner as a friend today?*

Explain that partners will work together again tomorrow.

EXTENSION

Create a Story About Your School

Start a drawing of your school building on a large sheet of chart paper. Encourage the students to tell more about the school by adding details and words to the drawing. Leave the drawing at a table for students to add to during the week. At the end of the week have a class "reading" of the picture.

Teacher Note

On Day 2, the students reread their stories and think about what they can add to their drawing and writing. If possible, have students who are not done writing at least one sentence and drawing a picture finish doing so before you teach the Day 2 lesson.

Save your shared story to use on Day 2.

Unit 3 ▶ Week 1

Day 2

Rereading and Telling More

Materials
- Shared story from Day 1
- Students' stories from Day 1

In this lesson, the students:
- Add to a shared story
- Reread and add to their writing
- Approximate spelling and use the word wall
- Capitalize the first letters of sentences and use periods at the ends
- Treat one another as friends

GETTING READY TO WRITE

1 Reread and Add to a Shared Story

Gather the class with partners sitting together, facing you. Remind the students that they chose their own topics and started writing stories yesterday. Also remind them that you stopped them during writing time to help them tell more by adding to their illustration. Explain that today the students will have a chance to tell more by adding to the words in their stories.

Direct the students' attention to yesterday's shared story and reread it aloud. Think aloud and model adding a sentence to the story; then ask:

Q *What words can I add to the illustration to tell more?*

Q *What else might I tell in this story? What sentence can I write to tell about that?*

Use the students' suggestions to add words to the illustration and one or two more sentences to the story. Be ready to restate the students' ideas as complete sentences, if necessary, before writing them.

> **Teacher Note**
> You might say, "When I reread this story, I thought of other things I could add to tell more. I remember that the duck was in the water looking for food. I'll add the sentence *He was looking for food* to the story."

> **Teacher Note**
> If the students have difficulty coming up with suggestions, remind them that they can look at the details in the illustration to help them think of writing ideas.

206 | Being a Writer™

Students might say:

"He was quacking. You can write *quack* on the picture."

"You can write *duck* in the picture."

"You can tell what color the duck was."

"You can write *He was brown with a green head.*"

As you write, point out that you are starting each sentence with a capital letter and ending it with a period. Also continue to look for opportunities to model approximating spelling and using the word wall.

2 Reread and Think About Telling More

Distribute the students' stories. Give them time to look carefully at their picture and read any words they wrote while pointing to each word and saying it aloud. Then use "Think, Pair, Share" to have partners first think about and then discuss:

 Q *What might you add to the words in your story to tell more?* [pause] *Turn to your partner.*

 Q *What words might you add to your picture to tell more?* [pause] *Turn to your partner.*

Telling More

Teacher Note

During this step, consider adding more high-frequency sight words to the word wall using the procedure you used in Unit 2, Week 6, Day 1 (see page 129). Refer to page 140 for a list of high-frequency sight words.

 **Note**

You might invite your English Language Learners to label their illustrations with words from their native languages.

Signal for the students' attention and have a few volunteers share what they plan to add.

Students might say:

"The sun was shining at the park. I'm going to write *The sun was shining*."

"My grandpa visited us, too. I'm going to write *Grandpa* on my picture."

"In my drawing, my dog is playing with a ball. I can write *ball* next to the ball."

Explain that you would like the students to add words (rather than more illustrations) to their stories today. Encourage them to use the ideas they shared with their partner to tell more in their stories.

WRITING TIME

3. Add Words to Stories to Tell More

Have the students return to their desks and work on adding to their stories. Remind them to use the word wall to spell words they've learned and to sound out unfamiliar words. Students who finish their story may start a new one or return to a previous story and add to it. As the students work, walk around and observe.

> **CLASS ASSESSMENT NOTE**
>
> Observe the students and ask yourself:
>
> - Are the students able to tell more by adding words and/or sentences to their writing and illustrations?
> - Are they able to communicate their ideas through drawing and writing?
> - Do they approximate spelling by sounding out unfamiliar words?
> - Do they leave spaces between words?
>
> *continues*

Unit 3 ▸ Week 1 ▸ Day 2 Telling More

> **CLASS ASSESSMENT NOTE** *continued*
>
> This first attempt at telling more may be challenging for students. This is to be expected. During the next few weeks, they will have multiple opportunities to practice adding to their writing and drawing. As they gain experience, their confidence and proficiency will build.

Signal to let the students know when writing time is over. Ask them to reread their stories; then ask and briefly discuss:

Q *What word wall words did you include in your writing? Read us a sentence where you used a word wall word.*

Q *Which words did you spell by sounding them out? How did you spell them?*

SHARING AND REFLECTING

4 Share Something They Like About Their Story and Reflect

Gather the class with partners sitting together, facing you. Have them bring their stories with them. Explain that today each student will choose something they like about their story and share it with their partner. Tell them that they can share something in their picture or their words. Give the students a few moments to choose what they like in their story; then have them share in pairs.

When most partners have finished talking, signal for their attention. Ask and briefly discuss:

Q *What did you hear or see that got you interested in your partner's story?*

Q *What did you do to be a good listener and friend during sharing time today?*

Collect the students' stories for sharing on Day 3.

Unit 3 ▸ Week 1

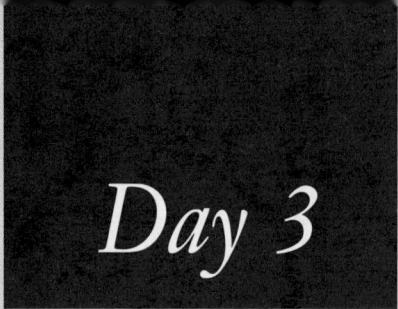

Day 3

Sharing as a Community

Materials

- Students' stories from Day 2

In this lesson, the students:

- Share stories as a community
- Speak clearly and listen to one another
- Learn the prompt "I found out" to express interest in one another's writing
- Treat one another as friends
- Write and draw freely

GETTING READY TO SHARE

1 ▶ Discuss Showing Interest in One Another's Writing

Gather the class with partners sitting together, facing you. Remind them that this week they wrote stories and thought about how they could tell more by adding to their pictures and words. Explain that today some of them will have the chance to share their stories with the class. Ask and briefly discuss:

Q *What do we do to show our classmates we are interested in their stories?*

Students might say:

"We are quiet when they are sharing."

"We look at them."

"We tell them what we liked about their stories."

"We ask them questions about their stories."

Explain that today the students will learn another way to show they are interested in one another's writing.

> **Teacher Note**
> If the students have difficulty answering this question, suggest some ideas like those in the "Students might say" note.

210 | Being a Writer™

▶ 2 Teach the Discussion Prompt "I Found Out"

Explain that today the students will learn to use the prompt "I found out" to help them say what they learned about another student from his story. Write the prompt *I found out _____* where everyone can see it. Point to the prompt and have the students read the words with you.

SHARING TIME

▶ 3 Share Stories and Use the Prompt "I Found Out"

Take a story from the pile of stories you collected on Day 2. Ask the author to stand next to you to share her story. Remind the author to read any words in a loud, clear voice and to show and explain her illustration to the class. When she finishes, ask the class to listen as you model using "I found out" to talk about the story.

Ask and briefly discuss:

Q *What did you find out from listening to [Tania's] story?*

Q *[Tania], how does it feel to know that we listened carefully to your story and learned something from it?*

Continue to have students share their stories. Remind them to use the prompt "I found out" as they comment on their classmates' stories. If necessary, have part of the class share now and plan another time for the rest of the class to share.

REFLECTING

▶ 4 Reflect on Using the Prompt "I Found Out" to Express Interest

Ask and briefly discuss:

Q *How did you do using the prompt "I found out" to show interest in other people's stories?*

◀ **Teacher Note**

You might say, "I found out that [Tania's] grandmother brought presents when she visited. That told me more about the visit."

◀ **Teacher Note**

Discussion prompts give the students more responsibility for the discussion when commenting on their classmates' writing. This allows you to step back from facilitating the discussion and simply observe once the students have become proficient in using the prompts.

Q *What is something you found out from a classmate's story today?*

Point out that using the prompt "I found out" to express interest in one another's writing is a way to treat one another as friends. The students will have more opportunities to practice using this prompt in the coming days.

FREE WRITING TIME

 Write and Draw Freely

Give the students time to write and draw about anything they choose. They may write about an idea from one of the writing ideas charts from Unit 2, or they may write about anything else. Tell the students to think quietly about what they might like to write, and then have partners turn to each other and share their ideas.

Have a few volunteers share their ideas with the class; then distribute writing/drawing paper and have the students write and draw freely.

Week 2 Overview

UNIT 3: TELLING MORE

Writing Focus

- Students contribute to shared stories and write their own.
- Students select their own topics for writing.
- Students visualize to get story ideas.
- Students reread their stories and tell more.
- Students approximate spelling and use the word wall.
- Students explore capitalizing the first letters of sentences and using periods at the ends.

Social Focus

- Students listen respectfully to the thinking of others and share their own.
- Students express interest in and appreciation for one another's writing.
- Students act in fair and caring ways.

DO AHEAD

- Prior to Day 1, review the writing ideas charts from Unit 2 and choose a topic, such as a memorable class event, to write about in a shared story (see the diagram on page 215 for an example).

- Prior to Day 1, prepare a sheet of chart paper so it looks like an enlarged version of the writing/drawing paper the students will use.

TEACHER AS WRITER

"In a mood of faith and hope my work goes on. A ream of fresh paper lies on my desk…. I am a writer and I take up my pen to write."
—Pearl S. Buck

This week, pick one of the words from the following list and jot down several associations you have with it.

- Orange
- Star
- Jealous
- Mermaid
- Dirt
- Address

Use your associations to write freely on the subject, incorporating new ideas as they occur to you. Make it your goal to fill several pages of your writing notebook.

Unit 3 ▶ Week 2

Day 1

Materials
- Writing ideas charts from Unit 2
- Chart paper (see "Do Ahead" on page 213) and a marker

Choosing Topics and Writing Stories

In this lesson, the students:

- Contribute to a shared story
- Visualize and write about topics that interest them
- Reread their stories and add to their illustrations
- Approximate spelling and use the word wall
- Capitalize the first letters of sentences and use periods at the ends

GETTING READY TO WRITE

1 Think About and Write a Shared Story

Gather the class with partners sitting together, facing you. Remind the students that they chose topics and wrote stories about those topics last week, and that they told more by adding to both their drawings and their words. Explain that they will practice this again this week.

Ask the students to watch as you review the writing ideas charts from Unit 2 and choose an idea (different from the idea you used last week) for a shared story. Think aloud about the story; then write the first sentence and draw a simple picture to start the story. As you write, point out that you are starting your sentence with a capital letter and you are ending it with a period.

 Note

The frequent charting and modeling of drawing and writing in this program supports English Language Learners as well as all beginning writers.

Unit 3 ▶ Week 2 ▶ Day 1 **Telling More**

Reread the story and explain that you would like the students' help to tell more about the story. Have the students close their eyes and make pictures in their minds as you ask questions like the ones that follow, one at a time. Pause between each question to give the students time to think.

Q *Where did we see the [fire truck]?*

Q *What did the [fire truck] look like?*

Q *Who else was there?*

Q *What did we see or hear around us?*

Have the students open their eyes. Use "Think, Pair, Share" to have partners first think about and then discuss:

 Q *What can we add to our picture to tell more about our story?* [pause] *Turn to your partner.*

Signal for the students' attention and have a few volunteers share their thinking with the class.

◀ **Teacher Note**
If the students have difficulty suggesting additional ideas, continue to think aloud and model adding to your illustration.

Kindergarten | 215

Students might say:

"The fire truck was next to the playground."

"The truck was red and had lights on top."

"The ladder on the truck went up."

"There were two firefighters."

"They were wearing yellow coats and pants."

Use the students' suggestions to add details to the picture. Retell the story to the students by reading the words and telling about the details in the picture. Point out how adding to the picture tells more about the story and makes it more interesting.

2 Visualize a Topic and Share Ideas

Explain that, as they did in Week 1, the students will choose a topic and write a story about it. Encourage them to choose a topic that is different from what they wrote about last week. Review the writing ideas charts from Unit 2 and remind them that they may write a story about one of the charted topics, if they wish. Give them a few moments to decide on a topic to write about.

Ask the students to close their eyes and think about the following questions as you ask them, one at a time. Pause between each question to give the students time to think.

Q *What are you going to write about today?*

Q *What's happening in your story?*

Q *Where is your story happening?*

Q *Who is in your story?*

Have the students open their eyes. Use "Think, Pair, Share" to have partners first think about and then discuss:

Q *What did you picture in your mind that you might write about today?* [pause] *Turn to your partner.*

Signal for the students' attention and have a few volunteers share their ideas with the class.

Students might say:

"We went to the zoo. I'm going to draw our class looking at the camels and write *zoo*."

"My cousin came to visit this weekend. I'll draw us playing basketball."

"My story is about the Chinese New Year parade. I'm going to draw a dragon."

Encourage the students to use the ideas they shared with their partner in their stories today.

Teacher Note

If you notice students having difficulty choosing a topic, stimulate their thinking by asking questions such as:

Q *What did you do today that was fun? What might you write about that?*

Q *Who is a friend you might write about?*

Q *What is something interesting we have done at school? What might you write about that?*

WRITING TIME

3 Write and Draw Stories

Have the students return to their seats, and distribute the writing/drawing paper. Encourage them to sound out words and use the word wall to help them with their spelling. When they have settled into their writing, begin conferring with individual students.

TEACHER CONFERENCE NOTE

During the next three weeks, confer with individual students by having each student tell you about his story, explain his drawing, and read any writing aloud. Ask yourself:

- Is the student able to choose an idea and begin writing or drawing a story?

- Is he adding to his picture or words to tell more about his story?

- Is he writing sentences? Words? Letters?

- Is he approximating spelling and/or using the word wall to help him write words?

continues

> **TEACHER CONFERENCE NOTE** *continued*
>
> Things you can do to support a student during a conference:
>
> - Ask him to visualize and tell you his story.
> - Ask him questions to elicit more ideas.
> - Approximate the spelling of unfamiliar words with him.
> - Point out words on the word wall.
> - If a student struggles to write anything at all, provide a sentence starter or transcribe the first few words of a story as the student dictates it; then have him copy what you wrote and continue writing and drawing on his own.
>
> Document your observations for each student using the "Conference Notes" record sheet (BLM1). Use the "Conference Notes" record sheets during conferences throughout this unit.

After 10–15 minutes, signal for the students' attention. Have them take a moment to reread their story and look at their illustration; then ask:

 Q *What can you add to your picture to tell more in your story?* [pause] *Turn to your partner.*

After partners have discussed the question, signal for their attention. Without discussing the question as a class, have the students resume their independent work. Encourage them to add to their pictures to tell more.

Signal to let the students know when writing time is over. Ask and briefly discuss:

Q *What did you add to your drawing after you talked to your partner?*

SHARING AND REFLECTING

4 Share Something They Like About Their Story and Reflect

Gather the class with partners sitting together, facing you. Have them bring their stories with them. Explain that, as they did last week, each student will choose something they like about their story and share it with their partner. Tell them they can share something in their picture or their words. Give the students a few moments to choose what they like in their story; then have them share in pairs.

After allowing sufficient time for partners to share their writing, signal for the students' attention and ask and briefly discuss:

Q *What did you hear or see that got you interested in your partner's story?*

Q *What did you do to be a good listener and friend during sharing time today?*

Collect the students' stories and tell the students that they will add more to their stories tomorrow.

Teacher Note
On Day 2, the students reread their stories and think about what they can add to their drawing and writing. If possible, have students who are not done writing at least one sentence and drawing a picture finish doing so before you teach the Day 2 lesson.

Save your shared story to use on Day 2.

EXTENSION

Practice Orally Telling More Using Wordless Picture Books

Have the students practice orally telling more using wordless picture books such as *Good Night, Gorilla* by Peggy Rathmann or *Pancakes for Breakfast* by Tomie dePaola. Page through the book and have partners turn and tell the story to each other by talking about what is happening in each illustration.

Unit 3 ▶ Week 2

Day 2

Rereading and Telling More

Materials
- Shared story from Day 1
- Students' stories from Day 1

In this lesson, the students:
- Add to a shared story
- Reread and add to their writing
- Approximate spelling and use the word wall
- Treat one another as friends

GETTING READY TO WRITE

1 Reread and Add to a Shared Story

Gather the class with partners sitting together, facing you. Remind the students that they chose their own topics and started writing stories yesterday. Also remind them that you stopped them during writing time to help them tell more by adding to their illustrations. Explain that today the students will have a chance to tell more by adding to the words in their stories.

Direct the students' attention to yesterday's shared story and reread it aloud. Think aloud and model adding a sentence to the story; then ask:

Q *What words can I add to the illustration to tell more?*

Q *What else might I tell in this story? What sentence can I write to tell about that?*

Use the students' suggestions to add words to the illustration and one or two more sentences to the story. Be ready to restate the students' ideas as complete sentences, if necessary, before writing them.

> **Teacher Note** ▶
> You might say, "When I reread this story, I thought of other things we could add to tell more. The firefighters told us all about the truck. I will add the sentence, *The firefighters told us about the truck.*"

> **Teacher Note** ▶
> If the students have difficulty coming up with suggestions, remind them that they can look at the details in the illustration to help them think of writing ideas.

220 | Being a Writer™

Students might say:

"The truck was red. You could write *red* on the picture."

"The firefighters were really funny. You can write *They were funny.*"

"You can write *It was a lot of fun.*"

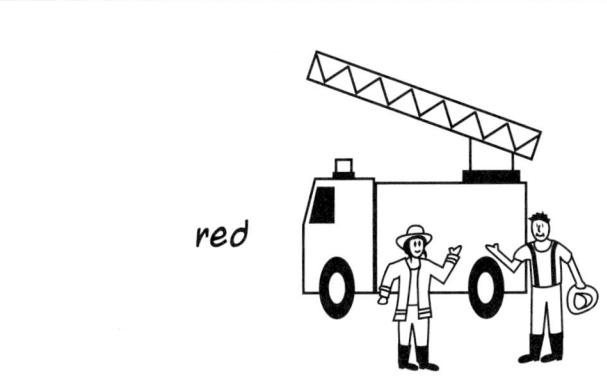

2 Reread and Think About Telling More

Distribute the students' stories. Give them time to look carefully at their pictures and read any words they wrote by pointing to each word and saying it aloud. Then use "Think, Pair, Share" to have partners first think about and then discuss:

 Q *What might you add to the words in your story to tell more?* [pause] *Turn to your partner.*

 Q *What words might you add to your picture to tell more?* [pause] *Turn to your partner.*

Signal for the students' attention and have a few volunteers share what they plan to add with the class.

Students might say:

"We saw snakes at the zoo. I'm going to write *We saw snakes*."

"We ate tacos after we played basketball. I'm going to write *We ate tacos*."

"In my drawing, I am watching the parade. I can write the word *me* on my picture."

Explain that you would like the students to add words (rather than more illustrations) to their stories today. Encourage them to use the ideas they shared with their partner to tell more in their stories today.

WRITING TIME

3 ▶ Add Words to Stories to Tell More

Have the students return to their desks and work on adding to their stories. Students who finish their story may start a new one or return to a previous story and add to it. Once the students have settled into their writing, confer with individual students.

TEACHER CONFERENCE NOTE

Continue to confer with individual students by having each student tell you about her story, explain her drawing, and read any writing. Ask yourself:

- Is the student able to choose an idea and begin writing or drawing a story?

- Is she adding to her picture or words to tell more about the story?

- Is she writing sentences? Words? Letters?

- Is she approximating spelling and/or using the word wall to help her write words?

continues

TEACHER CONFERENCE NOTE *continued*

Things you can do to support a student during a conference:

- Ask her to visualize and tell you her story.
- Ask her questions to elicit more ideas.
- Approximate the spelling of unfamiliar words with her.
- Point out words on the word wall.
- If a student struggles to write anything at all, provide a sentence starter or transcribe the first few words of a story as the student dictates it; then have her copy what you wrote and continue writing and drawing on her own.

Document your observations for each student using the "Conference Notes" record sheet (BLM1).

Signal to let the students know when writing time is over. Ask them to reread their stories; then ask and briefly discuss:

Q *What word wall words did you include in your writing? Read us a sentence where you used a word wall word.*

Q *Which words did you spell by sounding them out? How did you spell them?*

SHARING AND REFLECTING

 Share Additions to Stories

Gather the class with partners sitting together, facing you. Have the students bring their stories with them. Explain that partners will share what they added to their stories with each other. Tell them to listen carefully because you will ask them to share one thing their partner added with the class.

Telling More

**Note**

You might provide the prompt "My partner added…" to your English Language Learners to help them verbalize their answers to this question.

Give partners several minutes to share their stories. When most partners have finished sharing, signal for the students' attention and ask:

Q *What is one thing your partner added to his or her story today?*

Collect the students' stories for sharing on Day 3.

Unit 3 ▸ Week 2

Telling More

Day 3

Sharing as a Community

In this lesson, the students:

- Share stories as a community
- Speak clearly and listen to one another
- Learn the prompt "I want to know" to express interest in one another's writing
- Treat one another as friends
- Write and draw freely

Materials

- Students' stories from Day 2

GETTING READY TO SHARE

1 **Teach the Discussion Prompt "I Want to Know"**

Gather the class with partners sitting together, facing you. Explain that some of the students will share their writing with the class today. Remind them that last week they learned to use the prompt "I found out" to tell what they learned from a classmate's story. Explain that they will learn another prompt today to express interest in one another's writing.

Write the prompt *I want to know* _____ where everyone can see it. Point to the prompt and have the students read the words with you. Explain that you would like the students to use this prompt when they give comments after a classmate has shared.

Ask and briefly discuss:

Q *How do you think it would feel to have people tell you they want to know more about your story?*

FACILITATION TIP

Continue to practice **asking facilitative questions** to help the students respond to one another during class discussions. When students direct their responses to you, redirect them toward the class by asking questions like:

Q *Do you agree or disagree with what [Travis] just said, and why?*

Q *What can you add to what [Travis] said?*

Much learning in this program relies on creating a dynamic discourse among the students. Facilitative questions teach them that their comments contribute to a class discussion, and that they are responsible for listening to one another and responding.

Kindergarten | 225

Telling More   Unit 3 ▶ Week 2 ▶ Day 3

SHARING TIME

2 Share Stories and Model Using the Prompt "I Want to Know"

Take a story from the pile of stories you collected on Day 2. Ask the author to stand next to you to share the story. Remind the author to read any words in a loud, clear voice and to show and explain his illustration to the class. When he finishes, ask the class to listen as you model using the prompt "I want to know" to talk about the story.

Ask and briefly discuss:

Q *What else do you want to know about [Albert's] story?*

Q *[Albert], how does it feel to know that we listened carefully to your story and want to know more about it?*

Continue to have students share their stories. Remind them to use the prompt "I want to know" as they comment on the stories. If necessary, have part of the class share now and plan another time for the rest of the class to share.

> **Teacher Note**
>
> You might say, "I found out that [Albert] and his cousin like to eat tacos. I want to know where [Albert's] cousin was visiting from. That would tell me more about his story."

> **Teacher Note**
>
> The purpose of this question is to encourage the students to continue to think about how they can tell more in their writing. If they struggle to answer the question, model a response by telling the author something more you would like to know about his story. Then repeat the question.

CLASS ASSESSMENT NOTE

Observe the students as they share and discuss their writing as a class. Ask yourself:

- Does the student who is sharing read and talk in a loud, clear voice?
- Do the students listen carefully to one another?
- Do they use the prompt "I want to know" when they comment?

If necessary, stop the discussion to remind the students to use the prompt "I want to know" when giving their comments.

REFLECTING

Reflect on Using the Prompt "I Want to Know" to Express Interest

Ask and briefly discuss:

Q *How did you do using the prompt "I want to know" to show interest in other people's stories?*

Q *What is something you found out from a classmate's story today?*

Point out that using the prompt "I want to know" to express interest in one another's writing is a way to treat one another as friends. They will have more opportunities to practice the prompt "I want to know" in the coming days.

FREE WRITING TIME

Write and Draw Freely

Give the students time to write and draw about anything they choose. They may write about an idea on one of the writing ideas charts from Unit 2, or they may write about anything else. Ask the students to think quietly about what they might like to write and then have partners turn to each other and share their ideas.

Have a few volunteers share their ideas with the class; then distribute writing/drawing paper and have the students write and draw freely.

Week 3 Overview

UNIT 3: TELLING MORE

Cookie's Week
by Cindy Ward, illustrated by Tomie dePaola
(PaperStar, 1997)

There's no time to rest for this mischievous cat.

Unit 3 ▶ Week 3   Telling More

Writing Focus

- Students explore how a professional author tells more.
- Students explore how a professional illustrator tells more.
- Students reread their stories and tell more.
- Students approximate spelling and use the word wall.
- Students explore capitalizing the first letters of sentences and using periods at the ends.
- Students share their stories from the Author's Chair.

Social Focus

- Students learn procedures for working together.
- Students work in a responsible way.
- Students listen respectfully to the thinking of others and share their own.
- Students express interest in and appreciation for one another's writing.

DO AHEAD

- Prior to Day 1, consider previewing this week's read-aloud, *Cookie's Week*, with your English Language Learners. Read it aloud and show and discuss the illustrations, or have the students flip through it on their own.
- Prior to Day 1, prepare a transparency (or chart) of "On _____" (BLM6).
- Prior to Day 1, make a copy of "On _____" (BLM6) for each student.
- Prior to Day 2, make a copy of "On _____" (BLM6) for each student.

TEACHER AS WRITER

"If you want to learn how to write, write a lot and you will get better at it."
— Robert Munsch

This week, look through your writing notebook at some of your earlier drafts. Pick a sentence that you like, perhaps because of its sensory detail, dynamic action, or compelling subject matter. Write it at the top of a blank page and use it to begin a new piece of writing. If you get stuck, ask yourself questions using the words *who, what, when, where, why,* and *how* to keep writing.

Kindergarten | 229

Unit 3 ▶ Week 3

Day 1

Writing Stories

Materials
- *Cookie's Week*
- Transparency (or chart) of "On _____" (see "Do Ahead" on page 229)
- Overhead pen (or marker)
- Copies of "On _____" (see "Do Ahead" on page 229)

In this lesson, the students:
- Explore how a professional author tells more
- Contribute to a shared story
- Write about weekly activities
- Approximate spelling and use the word wall

GETTING READY TO WRITE

1 Read *Cookie's Week* Aloud

Gather the class with partners sitting together, facing you. Remind the students that they have been thinking about how to tell more in their stories by adding to their drawings and writing. This week they will write a story telling as much as they can; then they will share it with the class at the end of the week.

Show the cover of *Cookie's Week* and explain that you will read it aloud to help the students get ideas for their own writing. Read the title and the names of the author and illustrator aloud; then read the story aloud slowly and clearly, showing the illustrations and clarifying vocabulary as you read.

Making Meaning® Teacher

Your students will be familar with this book because it is used in *Making Meaning* Unit 4, Week 2. Remind them that they have heard the story and ask them what they remember about it. Explain that today they will hear the story again so that they can think about how the author wrote it.

> **Suggested Vocabulary**
> **windowsill:** shelf at the bottom of a window (p. 7)
> **upset:** knocked over (p. 11)
> **stuck:** trapped (p. 15)

Unit 3 ▸ Week 3 ▸ Day 1   **Telling More**

 Reread and Discuss How the Author Tells More

Ask and briefly discuss the following question. Be ready to reread from the story to help the students recall what they heard.

Q *What are some things Cookie does during the week?*

Show and reread pages 6–7; then point out that the author could have written, "On Tuesday…Cookie knocked a plant off the windowsill" and stopped there. Instead she tells more by describing what happens after Cookie knocks the plant off the windowsill. Show and reread pages 8–9; then continue rereading pages 10–13, pointing out that every time Cookie does something, the author always tells more about what happens afterward. By telling more, the author helps us get to know Cookie and makes the story more fun to read.

Tell the students that this week they are going to write a story about an activity they do during the week. Remind the students that they are going to think about how they can tell more, both in their pictures and in their words, as they write.

Making Meaning® Teacher

For more examples of stories that use repetitive language and tell more, you might reread these *Making Meaning* books to the students: *If You Give a Mouse a Cookie* and *I Was So Mad*.

 Write a Shared Story About a Monday Activity

Show the transparency of "On _____" (BLM6) on the overhead projector (or show the chart) and explain that you would like the class's help to write about an activity they do on Mondays. Write the word *Monday* on the blank and read the words *On Monday* aloud. Ask:

Q *What is an activity that our class does on Monday? Turn to your partner.*

After a moment, signal for the students' attention and have a few volunteers share their ideas with the class.

◂ **Teacher Note**

If you are teaching this lesson on a day other than Monday, consider using this day (for example, Tuesday) in the writing activity.

◂ **Teacher Note**

If the students have difficulty remembering what kinds of activities they do on Mondays, remind them of some and write them on the transparency.

Students might say:

"We write in our Monday journals."

"We get new spelling words."

"We go to the library."

"We read the morning message."

Kindergarten | 231

Telling More Unit 3 ▸ Week 3 ▸ Day 1

Use a student's suggestion to model writing a sentence and drawing a simple picture about an activity the class does on Mondays (for example, *On Monday…We go to the library*). Be ready to restate the students' ideas as complete sentences, if necessary, before writing them. Ask:

Q *What can we add to tell more about [going to the library]?*

Have a few volunteers share their ideas; then use a student's suggestion to add a sentence to the shared story (for example, *We look at books*). As you write, point out that you are starting your sentence with a capital letter and ending it with a period.

Explain that the students will write their own story about something they do on Monday. Tell them they may write about an activity they do in school or at home. Encourage them to tell as much as they can, using both pictures and words.

Teacher Note

If the students struggle to answer the question, stimulate their thinking by asking questions such as:

Q *What do we do when [we get to the library]?*

Q *Who helps us when we [go to the library]?*

Q *What happens after [we go to the library]?*

WRITING TIME

4. Write and Draw Stories

Have the students return to their seats, and distribute an "On _____" sheet to each student. Have them copy the word *Monday* from your transparency onto their own papers and then write and draw about an activity they do on Mondays. When they have settled into their writing, confer with individual students.

TEACHER CONFERENCE NOTE

Continue to confer with individual students by having each student tell you about his story, explain his drawing, and read any writing. Ask yourself:

- Is the student able to begin writing or drawing a story?
- Is he adding to his picture or words to tell more about his story?
- Is he writing sentences? Words? Letters?
- Is he approximating spelling and/or using the word wall to help him write words?

Things you can do to support a student during a conference:

- Ask him to visualize and tell you his story.
- Ask him questions to elicit more ideas.
- Approximate the spelling of unfamiliar words with him.
- Point out words on the word wall.
- If a student struggles to write anything at all, provide a sentence starter or transcribe the first few words of a story as the student dictates it; then have him copy what you wrote and continue writing and drawing on his own.

Document your observations for each student using the "Conference Notes" record sheet (BLM1).

After 10–15 minutes, signal for the students' attention. Have them take a moment to reread their story and look at their illustration; then ask:

 Q *What can you add to your picture or words to tell more in your story?* [pause] *Turn to your partner.*

After partners have discussed the question, signal for the students' attention. Without discussing the question as a class, have the students resume their independent work. Encourage them to add to their pictures and words to tell more.

Signal to let the students know when writing time is over. Ask and briefly discuss:

Q *What did you add to your story after you talked to your partner?*

SHARING AND REFLECTING

 5 Share Something They Like About Their Story and Reflect

Gather the class with partners sitting together, facing you. Have the students bring their stories with them. Explain that, as they did last week, each student will choose something they like about their story and share it with their partner. Tell them that they can share something in either their picture or their words. Give the students a few moments to choose what they like in their story; then have them share in pairs.

When most of the students have finished sharing, signal for their attention. Ask and briefly discuss:

Q *What did you hear or see that got you interested in your partner's story?*

Collect the students' stories, and tell the students that they will add more to their stories tomorrow.

Teacher Note

On Day 2, the students reread their stories and think about what they can add to their drawing and writing. If possible, have students who are not done writing at least one sentence and drawing a picture finish doing so before you teach the Day 2 lesson.

Save your shared story to use on Day 2.

Unit 3 ▶ Week 3

Telling More

Day 2

Rereading and Telling More

In this lesson, the students:

- Explore how a professional illustrator tells more
- Add to a shared story
- Reread and add to their stories
- Approximate spelling and use the word wall

Materials

- *Cookie's Week*
- Shared story from Day 1
- Students' stories from Day 1
- Copies of "On _____" (see "Do Ahead" on page 229)

GETTING READY TO WRITE

▶ 1 Explore Illustrations in *Cookie's Week*

Gather the class with partners sitting together, facing you. Show the cover of *Cookie's Week* and remind the students that they heard the story yesterday. Ask and briefly discuss:

Q *What do you remember about how the author, Cindy Ward, tells more about Cookie every day of the week?*

If necessary, remind the students that the author not only writes what Cookie does every day, but she also tells what happens afterward. Explain that the illustrator (the person who draws the pictures), Tomie dePaola, also tells more about the story using the drawings. Today the students will think about how he tells more in his pictures.

Show the illustration on pages 6–7 and reread the text aloud. Ask:

Q *What in the picture tells us that Cookie knocked a plant off the windowsill?*

Kindergarten | 235

Telling More Unit 3 ▶ Week 3 ▶ Day 2

Students might say:

"The plant is going to fall."

"Cookie is behind the plants."

"One plant looks different than the other ones."

"Cookie's paw is on the plant."

Show the illustration on pages 8–9 and reread the text aloud. Ask:

Q *What in the picture tells us that there was dirt everywhere?*

Students might say:

"The dirt is all over the floor."

"There are paw prints in the dirt."

Repeat this process with a few more illustrations in the book. Point out that Tomie dePaola includes lots of details in his drawings—such as trash on the floor, clothes everywhere, and Cookie's tail as he runs away—to help readers know what is happening and to make the pictures interesting and fun to look at.

2 Reread and Add to a Shared Story

Direct the students' attention to yesterday's shared story. Reread the story, pointing to each word as you read it, and describe the illustration. Think aloud and model adding words to the story and details to the drawing; then ask:

Q *What other details can we add to the picture to tell more?*

Q *What words can I add to the illustration to tell more?*

Q *What else might I tell in this story? What sentence can I write to tell about that?*

Use the students' suggestions to add words and details to the illustration and one or two more sentences to the story. Be ready to restate the students' ideas as complete sentences, if necessary, before writing them.

> **Teacher Note** ▶
>
> You might say, "When I reread this story, I thought of other things we could add to tell more. We can add a picture of a student looking at a book. I will draw a student and write the word *student* next to him. I will also add the sentence *We check out the books we want to read* to the story."

Unit 3 ▶ Week 3 ▶ Day 2

Telling More

Students might say:

"You can write the word *books* next to the bookshelves."

"You can write *We check out books.*"

"You can write *We like books.*"

3 Reread and Think About Adding to Stories

Distribute the students' stories. Give them time to look carefully at their pictures and read any words they wrote while pointing to each word and saying it aloud. Then use "Think, Pair, Share" to have partners first think about and then discuss:

 Q *What might you add to the words in your story to tell more?* [pause] *Turn to your partner.*

 Q *What words or details might you add to your picture to tell more?* [pause] *Turn to your partner.*

Signal for the students' attention and have a few volunteers share what they plan to add with the class.

Explain that during writing time you would like the students to tell more in their stories by adding words and details to their writing

Teacher Note

Listen as partners share. If the students struggle to think of ideas, signal for their attention and have a volunteer share her story and drawing with the class. Think aloud about one or two things the student might add to her drawing. Then ask and briefly discuss as a class:

Q *What else might [Sara] add to her picture?*

If necessary, repeat the process with another volunteer.

Kindergarten | 237

and pictures. If they finish, they will get another "On _____" sheet and write about something they do on another day of the week. Write the names of the days of the week where everyone can see them.

WRITING TIME

4 Add to Stories to Tell More

Have the students return to their desks and work on adding to their stories. Students who finish their story should get a new "On _____" sheet and start writing about another day of the week. Once the students have settled into their writing, confer with individual students.

> **TEACHER CONFERENCE NOTE**
>
> Continue to confer with individual students by having each student tell you about her story, explain her drawing, and read any writing. Ask yourself:
>
> - Is the student able to add to her picture and words to tell more about the story?
> - Is she writing sentences? Words? Letters?
> - Is she approximating spelling and/or using the word wall to help her write words?
>
> Things you can do to support a student during a conference:
>
> - Ask her to visualize and tell you her story.
> - Ask her questions to elicit more ideas.
> - Approximate the spelling of unfamiliar words with her.
> - Point out words on the word wall.
>
> *continues*

> **TEACHER CONFERENCE NOTE** *continued*
>
> - If a student struggles to write anything at all, provide a sentence starter or transcribe the first few words of a story as the student dictates it; then have her copy what you wrote and continue writing and drawing on her own.
>
> Document your observations for each student using the "Conference Notes" record sheet (BLM1).

Signal to let the students know when writing time is over. Ask the students to reread their stories; then ask and briefly discuss:

Q *What word wall words did you include in your writing? Read us a sentence where you used a word wall word.*

Q *Which words did you spell by sounding them out? How did you spell them?*

SHARING

 Share Additions to Stories

Have a few volunteers share something they added to their stories.

Explain that tomorrow the students will have a chance to share their stories with the class. Collect their stories for Author's Chair sharing on Day 3.

Unit 3 ▶ Week 3

Day 3

Author's Chair Sharing

Materials

- A chair to use for the Author's Chair
- Students' stories from Day 2

In this lesson, the students:

- Learn the procedures for Author's Chair sharing
- Speak clearly and listen to one another
- Use the prompts "I found out" and "I want to know"
- Write and draw freely

About Author's Chair Sharing

This week, the students begin to share their writing from the Author's Chair. They will use the Author's Chair whenever they share their writing as a community in the future. The intention of Author's Chair sharing is to give each author "center stage" and to create a special atmosphere when students share their writing. Designate a special chair to be the Author's Chair, and plan to sit in the audience during Author's Chair sharing instead of next to the author. This allows each author to have everyone's full attention as he reads his story aloud and calls on classmates to receive feedback. While you will continue to facilitate the sharing and discussion from your seat in the audience, the idea is to do so with a lighter touch in order to build the students' sense of autonomy when sharing their writing.

GETTING READY TO SHARE

 Introduce the Author's Chair

Gather the class with partners sitting together, facing the Author's Chair. Direct the students' attention to the chair and explain that the students will share their writing from it for the rest of the year. Tell the students that you will join the audience during Author's Chair sharing. The author will sit in the chair and read his writing to the class, and then he will call on his classmates who want to comment on or ask questions about his story.

Point out that, because you will be in the audience, the students will need to take responsibility for making Author's Chair sharing go well. Briefly discuss:

Q *What will the author need to remember to do when he or she reads?*

Q *If you can't hear the author, what can you say or do to politely let him or her know?*

Q *What will you do to be a good audience member during Author's Chair sharing?*

Students might say:

"The author should wait until everyone is quiet before reading."

"The author should read in a loud voice."

"I can raise my hand and ask the author to please speak louder."

"The audience should be quiet when the author is reading."

"The audience should ask the author questions after he finishes reading."

2 Review the Prompts "I Found Out" and "I Want to Know"

Review the prompts "I found out" and "I want to know," and write them where everyone can see them. Explain that you would like the students to use the prompts when they comment on their classmates' stories today.

Explain that you will check in with the students later to see how they did.

SHARING TIME

3 Share from the Author's Chair

Call on a student to share his story from the Author's Chair. Remind the student to introduce himself as the author and illustrator, to show his illustration, and to read and tell about his story in a loud, clear voice.

FACILITATION TIP

Continue to **ask facilitative questions** to build accountability and participation during class discussions. Redirect students' comments to the class by asking:

Q *Do you agree or disagree with what [Ricki] just said, and why?*

Q *Why does what [Ricki] said make sense?*

Take your seat in the audience and have the student share. At the end of the sharing, lead the audience in clapping; then wait quietly until students begin to raise their hands to comment. If students do not raise their hands to comment after 15–20 seconds, raise your hand and comment on something you found out or something you want to know about the author's story (for example, "I found out that [Emilio] gets ready for school on Monday" or "I want to know what kind of cereal [Emilio] likes to eat"). If necessary, ask the class:

Q *What did you find out from listening to [Emilio's] story?*

Q *What do you want to know about [Emilio's] story?*

Allow the author to call on two or three students who would like to comment on his story. Follow this same procedure to have other students share from the Author's Chair.

CLASS ASSESSMENT NOTE

Observe the students as they share and discuss their writing as a class. Ask yourself:

- Does the student who is sharing read and talk in a loud, clear voice?
- Do the students listen to one another?
- Do they use the prompts "I found out" and "I want to know" when they comment?
- Are they able to carry out the Author's Chair sharing with minimal facilitation by me?
- What problems do I notice that I want to bring up during the reflection?

If necessary, stop the discussion to remind the students to use the prompts "I found out" and "I want to know" when giving their comments.

If you run out of time before all of the students have a chance to share, explain that you will plan another time to continue the Author's Chair sharing so everyone will get to share.

Teacher Note

Typically, only part of the class will get to share from the Author's Chair in any one sitting. Plan time before starting Week 4 for the rest of the students to share their stories from the Author's Chair.

REFLECTING

 Reflect on Author's Chair Sharing

Without mentioning students' names, report some observations (both successes and problems) you had during Author's Chair sharing. (You might say, "I noticed that several of you had comments about the stories. That shows me you were listening carefully when the authors shared. I noticed that I had to remind you several times to use the prompts 'I found out' and 'I want to know' when commenting on your classmates' stories.") Then ask:

Q *What else did you do to help make Author's Chair sharing go well today?*

Q *What other problems did you notice during Author's Chair sharing? What can you do next time to avoid those problems?*

Explain that the students will have more opportunities to share writing from the Author's Chair.

FREE WRITING TIME

 Write and Draw Freely

Give the students time to write and draw about anything they choose. They may write about an idea from one of the writing ideas charts from Unit 2, or they may write about anything else. Ask the students to think quietly about what they might like to write, and then have partners turn to each other and share their ideas.

Have a few volunteers share their ideas with the class; then distribute writing/drawing paper and have the students write and draw freely.

EXTENSION

Make Individual Books About Weekly Activities

Have the students write an "On _____" page for every day of the week; then compile each student's pages into a book. On the cover, have them write their own name in the title _____'s Week (for example, *Emily's Week* or *Tran's Week*). Plan time for students to share their books with the class from the Author's Chair.

Week 4 Overview

UNIT 3: TELLING MORE

When Sophie Gets Angry—Really, Really Angry...
by Molly Bang
(Scholastic Inc., 2004)

When Sophie and her sister have a disagreement, Sophie gets very angry.

Writing Focus

- Students explore how a professional author tells more.
- Students reread their stories and tell more.
- Students approximate spelling and use the word wall.
- Students explore capitalizing the first letters of sentences and using periods at the ends.
- Students share their stories from the Author's Chair.

Social Focus

- Students work in a responsible way.
- Students act in fair and caring ways.
- Students listen respectfully to the thinking of others and share their own.
- Students express interest in one another's writing.

DO AHEAD

- Prior to Day 1, consider previewing this week's read-aloud, *When Sophie Gets Angry—Really, Really Angry…*, with your English Language Learners. Read it aloud and show and discuss the illustrations, or have the students flip through it on their own. (See page 249 for suggested ELL vocabulary.)

TEACHER AS WRITER

"It would not hurt that we live our lives with childlike wonder. Have you asked yourself lately: 'When was the last time I saw something for the first time?'"
— Cecilia Borromeo

This week, write a "day in the life" piece, including everything you can think of that is happening at this moment. Try to write about events as if you are experiencing them "for the first time." Include both things that are happening in your immediate vicinity and larger, more impersonal events such as weather or politics. Try to fill several pages in your writing notebook.

Unit 3 ▶ Week 4

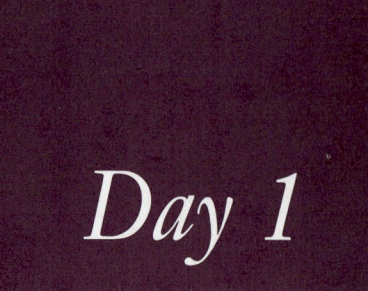

Day 1

Materials

- *When Sophie Gets Angry— Really, Really Angry…*
- *Cookie's Week* from Week 3
- (Optional) Chart paper and a marker

Writing Stories

In this lesson, the students:

- Explore how a professional author tells more
- Write about what they do when they get really angry
- Approximate spelling and use the word wall

GETTING READY TO WRITE

 Read *When Sophie Gets Angry—Really, Really Angry…* Aloud

Gather the class with partners sitting together, facing you. Show the cover of *Cookie's Week* and remind the students that last week they practiced telling more by writing stories about different activities they do during the week. This week, they will write a new story to share with the class at the end of the week.

Show the cover of *When Sophie Gets Angry—Really, Really Angry…* and explain that you will read it aloud to help the students get ideas for their own writing. Read the title and the name of the author aloud. Tell the students that the author, Molly Bang, is also the book's illustrator. Read the book aloud slowly and clearly, showing the illustrations and clarifying vocabulary as you read.

Making Meaning® Teacher

Your students will be familiar with this book because it is used in *Making Meaning* Unit 2, Week 1. Remind them that they have heard the story and ask them what they remember about it. Explain that today they will hear the story again so that they can think about how the author wrote it.

Suggested Vocabulary

snatched: grabbed quickly (p. 5)
smithereens: tiny pieces (p. 9)
volcano: mountaintop that blows out lava and ashes (p. 12)
explode: blow up (p. 12)
beech tree: kind of tree (p. 20)
comforts her: makes her feel better (p. 25)

248 | Being a Writer™

Unit 3 ▶ Week 4 ▶ Day 1   Telling More

ELL Vocabulary

English Language Learners may benefit from discussing additional vocabulary, including:

roars: makes a loud, deep sound, like a lion (p. 10)

2 Reread and Discuss How the Author Tells More

Ask and briefly discuss the questions that follow. Be ready to reread from the story to help the students recall what they heard.

Q *What did you find out about Sophie?*

Q *What helps Sophie calm down and stop feeling angry?*

Students might say:

"She gets very, very mad."

"She yells and screams really loud."

"She runs away. Then she cries."

"She goes outside. It is pretty there so she isn't angry anymore."

"She sits in a tree and forgets about being mad."

Show and reread pages 6–7 aloud. Point out that the author could have stopped after she wrote, "Oh, is Sophie ever angry now!" Instead, she tells more by describing what Sophie does when she gets angry. Continue showing and rereading pages 8–14. Ask and briefly discuss:

Q *What does Sophie do when she gets angry?*

Students might say:

"She kicks and screams."

"She wants to smash things."

"She runs."

Point out that by telling more the author helps us get to know Sophie and makes the story more interesting to read.

Tell the students that this week they are going to write a story about what they do when they get really angry. Remind the students that

Kindergarten | 249

they are going to think about how they can tell more, both in their pictures and their words, as they write.

 ### Visualize a Story and Share Ideas

Ask the students to close their eyes and picture in their mind a time when they were angry. Ask the following questions, one at a time, pausing between each question to give the students time to think.

> **Q** *Think about a time you were really, really angry like Sophie. What did you do?*

> **Q** *What do you look like when you're angry?*

> **Q** *What do you sound like?*

> **Q** *What helps you calm down?*

Have the students open their eyes. Use "Think, Pair, Share" to have partners first think about and then discuss:

 > **Q** *What did you picture in your mind that you might write about today?* [pause] *Turn to your partner.*

Signal for the students' attention and have a few volunteers share their ideas with the class.

Encourage the students to use the ideas they shared with their partner as they write their stories today.

Teacher Note

If you notice students having difficulty generating ideas for their stories, call for their attention and write a story together as a class using the procedure you used in Week 3, Day 1, Step 3 (see pages 231–232).

WRITING TIME

 ### Write and Draw Stories

Have partners sit together at desks, and distribute writing/drawing paper to each student. When they have settled into their writing, confer with individual students.

Unit 3 ▸ Week 4 ▸ Day 1 **Telling More**

TEACHER CONFERENCE NOTE

Continue to confer with individual students by having each student tell you about his story, explain his drawing, and read any writing. Ask yourself:

- Is the student able to begin writing or drawing a story?
- Is he adding to his picture or words to tell more about his story?
- Is he writing sentences? Words? Letters?
- Is he approximating spelling and/or using the word wall to help him write words?

Continue to support students during the conference using the suggestions that appear in the Teacher Conference Notes in Week 3 (see pages 238–239).

Document your observations for each student using the "Conference Notes" record sheet (BLM1).

After 10–15 minutes, signal for the students' attention. Have the students take a moment to reread their story and look at their illustration; then ask:

 Q *What can you add to your picture or words to tell more in your story?* [pause] *Turn to your partner.*

After allowing sufficient time for partners to discuss the question, signal for their attention. Without discussing the question as a class, have the students resume their independent work. Encourage them to add to their pictures and words to tell more.

Signal to let the students know when writing time is over. Ask and briefly discuss:

Q *What did you add to your story after you talked to your partner?*

Kindergarten | 251

SHARING AND REFLECTING

 Share Something They Like About Their Story and Reflect

Gather the class with partners sitting together, facing you. Have the students bring their stories with them. Explain that each student will choose something they like about their story and share it with their partner. Tell them that they can share something in either their picture or their words. Give the students a few moments to choose what they like in their story; then have them share in pairs.

When all of the students have shared, signal for their attention. Ask and briefly discuss:

Q *What did you hear or see that got you interested in your partner's story?*

Collect the students' stories, and tell the students that they will add more to their stories tomorrow.

Teacher Note

On Day 2, the students reread their stories and think about what they can add to their drawing and writing. If possible, have students who are not done writing at least one sentence and drawing a picture finish doing so before you teach the Day 2 lesson.

Unit 3 ▶ Week 4

Telling More

Day 2

Rereading and Telling More

In this lesson, the students:

- Explore how illustrations tell more
- Reread and add to their stories
- Approximate spelling and use the word wall

About Adding Speech and Sound Words to Illustrations

In previous units, the students learned to add labels to their illustrations. This lesson provides an informal introduction to adding spoken words and sound words to illustrations. The students are not expected to apply this skill to their writing now, though some may. In later units, they will have more opportunities to explore adding words like these to their stories.

Materials
- *When Sophie Gets Angry—Really, Really, Angry…*
- Students' stories from Day 1

GETTING READY TO WRITE

1 **Explore Illustrations in *When Sophie Gets Angry—Really, Really, Angry…***

Gather the class with partners sitting together, facing you. Show the cover of *When Sophie Gets Angry—Really, Really, Angry…* and remind the students that they heard the story yesterday. Ask and briefly discuss:

Q *What does the author, Molly Bang, tell us more about what happens when Sophie gets angry?*

If necessary, page through the story and remind the students that the author describes many different things that Sophie does when she gets angry. Explain that the illustrations also tell more about the story.

Show the illustrations on pages 2–3 and reread the text aloud. Point to the words *MY TURN*, and explain that Molly Bang wrote the words *MY TURN* next to Sophie's sister to show what the sister said when

Kindergarten | 253

Telling More   Unit 3 ▸ Week 4 ▸ Day 2

she grabbed Gorilla. Show and reread page 4, pointing to the word *NO* and explaining that it shows what Sophie said.

Explain that Molly Bang also added sound words to her pictures to make the pictures interesting. Show pages 9–14, pointing out the words *SMASH*, *ROAR*, *EXPLODE*, and *PABAM*.

2 Reread and Think About Adding to Stories

Distribute the students' stories. Give them time to look carefully at their pictures and read any words they wrote while pointing to each word and saying it aloud. Then use "Think, Pair, Share" to have partners first think about and then discuss:

Q *What words might you add to your picture to tell more?* [pause] *Turn to your partner.*

Q *What other words or details might you add to tell more in your story?* [pause] *Turn to your partner.*

Signal for the students' attention and have a few volunteers share what they plan to add with the class.

Explain that during writing time you would like the students to tell more in their stories by adding words and details to their writing and pictures.

ELL Note
You might invite your English Language Learners to add words in their native languages to their drawings.

WRITING TIME

3 Add to Stories to Tell More

Have the students return to their desks and work on adding to their stories. Students who finish early may get another sheet of paper and write about anything they choose. As the students write, walk around the room and observe.

Unit 3 ▶ Week 4 ▶ Day 2   Telling More

CLASS ASSESSMENT NOTE

Observe the students and ask yourself:

- Are the students able to tell more by adding words and/or sentences to their writing and illustrations?
- Are they able to communicate their ideas through drawing and writing?
- Do they approximate spelling by sounding out unfamiliar words?

If you notice students having difficulty adding to their writing, ask them questions such as:

Q *What do your [hands, feet, eyes] do when you are angry? What can you draw to show that?*

Q *What do you do to make yourself feel better? What word or sentence can you write to describe that?*

Q *Who do you talk to when you are angry? What can you write or draw to tell about that?*

Signal to let the students know when writing time is over. Ask the students to reread their stories; then ask and briefly discuss:

Q *What word wall words did you include in your writing? Read us a sentence where you used a word wall word.*

Q *Which words did you spell by sounding them out? How did you spell them?*

SHARING

 Share Additions to Stories

Have a few volunteers share what they added to their stories.

Explain that tomorrow more students will have a chance to share their stories from the Author's Chair. Collect their stories for sharing on Day 3.

Kindergarten | 255

EXTENSION

Discuss a Poem About Feeling Upset

Explain that you are going to read a poem called "Keziah" by Gwendolyn Brooks (*Read-Aloud Rhymes for the Very Young*, page 86). Have the students close their eyes and listen to the poem as you read it aloud slowly and clearly. Ask and discuss as a class:

Q *What does the person in the poem do when she is upset?*

Q *What do you do to make yourself feel better when you are upset?*

Unit 3 ▸ Week 4

Telling More

Day 3

Author's Chair Sharing

In this lesson, the students:

- Practice the procedures for Author's Chair sharing
- Speak clearly and listen to one another
- Use the prompts "I found out" and "I want to know"
- Treat one another as friends
- Write and draw freely

Materials
- Author's Chair
- Students' stories from Day 2

GETTING READY TO SHARE

1 Review Author's Chair Sharing

Gather the class with partners sitting together, facing the Author's Chair. Remind them that they wrote and told more in stories about what they do when they get angry. Explain that today some of the students will share their stories from the Author's Chair. Ask:

Q *What do you remember about what happens during Author's Chair sharing?*

Q *What will you do to be responsible when you share your writing from the Author's Chair?*

Q *What will you do to be responsible when you are a member of the audience?*

◀ **Teacher Note**

If necessary, remind the students of the procedures you would like them to follow when they share from the Author's Chair.

2 Review the Prompts "I Found Out" and "I Want to Know"

Review the prompts "I found out" and "I want to know" and write them where everyone can see them. Explain that you would like

Kindergarten | 257

Telling More — Unit 3 ▸ Week 4 ▸ Day 3

the students to use the prompts when they comment on their classmates' stories today.

Explain that you will check in with the students later to see how they did.

SHARING TIME

3 ▸ Share from the Author's Chair

Call on a student to share her story from the Author's Chair. Remind the student to introduce herself as the author and illustrator, to show her illustration, and to read and tell about her story in a loud, clear voice.

Take your seat in the audience and have the student share. At the end of the sharing, lead the audience in clapping; then wait quietly until students begin to raise their hands to comment. If students do not raise their hands to comment after 15–20 seconds, raise your hand and comment on something you found out or something you want to know about the author's story (for example, "I found out that [Thuy] slams the door when she's angry" or "I want to know where [Thuy] goes when she's angry"). If necessary, ask the class:

Q *What did you find out from listening to [Thuy's] story?*

Q *What do you want to know about [Thuy's] story?*

Allow the author to call on two or three students who would like to comment on her story. Follow this same procedure to have other students share from the Author's Chair. Explain that all of the students will have a chance to share from the Author's Chair in the coming days.

Teacher Note ▸

Plan time before starting Unit 4 for the rest of the students to share their stories from the Author's Chair.

REFLECTING

Reflect on Author's Chair Sharing

Ask and briefly discuss:

Q *What did you do to be responsible during Author's Chair sharing today?*

Q *When you act responsibly, you are treating others respectfully, as friends. What else did you do to treat your classmates as friends today?*

Q *What problems did you notice during Author's Chair sharing? What can you do next time to avoid those problems?*

Encourage the students to continue to think of ways to be responsible and to treat one another as friends throughout the school day.

FACILITATION TIP

Reflect on your experience over the past few weeks with **asking facilitative questions**. Does this technique feel comfortable and natural for you? Do you find yourself using it throughout the school day? What effect has using this technique had on your students' listening and participation in discussions? We encourage you to continue to use and reflect on this technique throughout the year.

FREE WRITING TIME

Write and Draw Freely

Give the students time to write and draw about anything they choose. They may write about an idea on one of the writing ideas charts from Unit 2, or they may write about anything else. Tell the students to think quietly about what they might like to write and then have partners turn to each other and share their ideas.

Have a few volunteers share their ideas with the class; then distribute writing/drawing paper and have the students write and draw freely.

Teacher Note

This is the last week of Unit 3. You will need to reassign partners for Unit 4.

Unit 4

Just the Facts

Unit 4

Just the Facts

During this three-week unit, the students hear and discuss nonfiction books and write nonfiction as a class and individually. They explore how nonfiction is different from fiction and write about their classroom, their partner, and food. They review approximating spelling and continue to explore writing and punctuating sentences. Socially, they make decisions together, work responsibly, and act in fair and caring ways. They share their writing in pairs and with the class from the Author's Chair.

UNIT OVERVIEW

WEEK	DAY 1	DAY 2	DAY 3
1	**Exploring Nonfiction:** *Airport* **Focus:** • Exploring nonfiction about a place • Making decisions together	**Writing Nonfiction** **Focus:** • Generating facts about the classroom • Writing/drawing facts about the classroom • Writing and punctuating sentences	**Author's Chair Sharing** **Focus:** • Expressing interest in one another's writing • Writing and drawing freely
2	**Exploring Nonfiction:** *Mr. Santizo's Tasty Treats!* **Focus:** • Exploring nonfiction about a person • Writing and drawing freely	**Writing Nonfiction** **Focus:** • Interviewing their partner • Writing/drawing a fact about their partner • Writing and punctuating sentences	**Writing Nonfiction and Sharing** **Focus:** • Interviewing and writing about their partner • Writing and punctuating sentences • Expressing interest in one another's writing
3	**Exploring Nonfiction:** *I Like Pasta* **Focus:** • Exploring nonfiction about a food • Writing and drawing freely	**Writing Nonfiction** **Focus:** • Observing and generating facts about a food • Writing/drawing facts about a food • Writing and punctuating sentences	**Writing Nonfiction and Sharing** **Focus:** • Observing and generating facts about a food • Writing facts about a food • Sharing writing in pairs

Week 1 Overview

UNIT 4: JUST THE FACTS

Airport
by Byron Barton
(HarperTrophy, 1987)

The airport bustles with activity from arrival to takeoff.

Writing Focus

- Students hear, discuss, and explore nonfiction books.
- Students generate a list of facts about the classroom.
- Students write and draw a fact about the classroom for a class book.
- Students write and punctuate sentences.
- Students review approximating spelling and using the word wall.

Social Focus

- Students build on one another's thinking.
- Students act in fair and caring ways.
- Students make decisions and solve problems respectfully.
- Students express interest in and appreciation for one another's writing.

DO AHEAD

- Prior to Day 1, decide how you will randomly assign partners to work together during this unit. See the front matter in volume 1 for suggestions about assigning partners randomly (page xiii) and for considerations for pairing English Language Learners (page xxvi).

- Prior to Day 1, collect enough nonfiction books so that each pair has one. Choose books on a variety of subjects (for example, people, places, animals, science, sports) at the various reading levels of your students. In addition, display *Cookie's Week* and one or two other fiction books the students have heard this year.

- Prior to Day 1, consider previewing this week's read-aloud, *Airport*, with your English Language Learners. Read it aloud and show and discuss the illustrations, or have the students flip through it on their own. (See page 268 for suggested ELL vocabulary.)

TEACHER AS WRITER

"I like to come away from reading a book with the feeling that I've learned something. That's why I like nonfiction."
— Gail Gibbons

Select a place that is special to you and write a list of facts about it (for example, what the place looks like and what you do there). Use the list to write a description of the place and share your writing with a friend or colleague. After sharing your writing, have your friend or colleague tell you what he or she learned about your special place.

Unit 4 ▶ Week 1

Day 1

Materials

- *Airport*
- *Cookie's Week* from Unit 3
- 1–2 other fiction books from earlier in the year (see "Do Ahead" on page 265)
- Collected nonfiction books (see "Do Ahead" on page 265)
- Self-stick note for each pair

Making Meaning® Teacher

You can either have the students work with their *Making Meaning* partner or assign them a different partner for the writing lessons.

Teacher Note

This lesson may require an extended class period.

Exploring Nonfiction

In this lesson, the students:

- Work with a new partner
- Explore the difference between fiction and nonfiction
- Hear and discuss a nonfiction book
- Share materials fairly
- Reach agreement before making decisions

About Nonfiction Writing in Kindergarten

In this unit, the students explore nonfiction books and learn that nonfiction writing gives facts about real-world topics. They hear and discuss books about a place (an airport), a person (a baker), and a food (pasta) and do their own nonfiction writing about a special place (their classroom), a special person (their partner), and special foods (grapes and raisins). They collect facts for their writing by observing and asking questions, and they build on the work they have done in previous units by writing longer pieces.

GETTING READY TO READ

1 Pair Students and Discuss Working Together

Randomly assign partners (see "Do Ahead" on page 265) and make sure they know each other's names. Gather the class with partners sitting together, facing you. Remind the students that they have written lots of stories and worked with several partners this year. Ask and briefly discuss:

Q *What will you do to treat your new partner as a friend today?*

Students might say:

"I'll look at my partner when we are sharing."

"I'll listen to my partner's ideas."

"I will smile and be nice to my partner."

Encourage the students to keep these ideas in mind as they work with their new partner today.

266 | Being a Writer™

Unit 4 ▶ Week 1 ▶ Day 1   **Just the Facts**

 Briefly Introduce Nonfiction Writing

Direct the students' attention to *Cookie's Week* and the other fiction books you displayed. Read the titles aloud, and point out that these are stories about *imaginary*, or made-up, people, places, or animals. For example, *Cookie's Week* is a story about a cat that makes messes around the house. Explain that made-up stories are called *fiction*.

Tell the students that today you are going to read them a different kind of book—a *nonfiction* book—which tells true information about real things. Invite the students to think about how today's read-aloud book is different from books like *Cookie's Week*.

3 **Introduce and Read *Airport* Aloud**

Show the cover of *Airport* and read the title and the author's name aloud. Ask and briefly discuss:

Q *What do you know, or think you know, about airports?*

Q *Who has been to an airport? Tell us about it.*

Read the book aloud slowly and clearly, showing the illustrations and stopping as described below. Clarify vocabulary as you read.

> **Suggested Vocabulary**
>
> **cockpit:** place at the front of the plane where the pilot sits (p. 18)
> **pilots:** people who fly the plane (p. 19)
> **control tower:** building from which people give instructions to pilots (p. 20)
> **radios:** sends a message (p. 20)
> **flight attendant:** person who helps passengers during the flight (p. 23)
> **runway:** long, flat area on the ground where airplanes take off and land (p. 25)

 **Note**

You might provide the prompts "I know" and "I think I know" to your English Language Learners to help them verbalize their answers to this question.

Kindergarten | 267

Just the Facts Unit 4 ▶ Week 1 ▶ Day 1

> **ELL Vocabulary**
>
> English Language Learners may benefit from discussing additional vocabulary, including:
>
> **cargo hold:** place on the plane where suitcases are kept during the flight (p. 12)
>
> **fuel:** gas (p. 13)
>
> **go on board:** get on the plane (p. 15)
>
> **all is clear:** it is safe for the plane to leave (p. 21)
>
> **takeoff:** leaving (p. 27)

Stop after:

p. 11 "…get loaded and checked."

Ask and briefly discuss:

Q *What have you learned from this book so far?*

Have a few volunteers share their answers. As they share, show the corresponding pages to the class.

> **Students might say:**
>
> "People go to the airport in cars."
>
> "They fly on jet planes."
>
> "They wait in the waiting room."

Reread the sentence on pages 8–11 and continue reading. Stop after:

p. 19 "…the pilots get ready."

Ask:

Q *What new things have you learned? Turn to your partner.*

After a moment, signal for the students' attention and have a few volunteers share their thinking with the class. As they share, show the corresponding pages to the class.

> **Students might say:**
>
> "Fuel goes in the wings of the plane."
>
> "People find their seats."
>
> "The pilots get ready."

Teacher Note ▶

If the students have trouble recalling what they heard, reread pages 3–11.

Students may want to share stories about their own experiences at the airport rather than reporting facts from the book. If this happens, gently redirect their thinking to the text.

Reread the sentence on pages 18–19 and continue reading to the end of the book.

Ask:

 Q *What new information have you learned? Turn to your partner.*

Again, signal for the students' attention and have a few volunteers share their thinking with the class. As they share, show the corresponding pages.

4 Briefly Discuss the Reading

Ask and briefly discuss:

Q *How is* Airport *different from a book like* Cookie's Week?

Students might say:

"*Cookie's Week* is about a make-believe cat."

"*Airport* is about something real."

"*Cookie's Week* tells a story, and *Airport* tells facts."

Emphasize that nonfiction books like *Airport* are not made-up stories like *Cookie's Week*. Instead, they give lots of interesting *facts* (or true information) to help us learn about a topic. Tell the students that today they will have a chance to look at some other nonfiction books.

Teacher Note

If the students have difficulty answering this question, suggest some ideas like those in the "Students might say" note, and then ask for other ideas.

 **Note**

You might simplify this question by asking:

Q *Airport and* Cookie's Week *are different kinds of books. How are they different?*

READING TIME

5 Model Exploring a Nonfiction Book

Direct the students' attention to the nonfiction books you collected. Explain that each pair will get a nonfiction book, and that partners will look at and talk about the pictures in the book. Tell them that, after they look through all the pictures, partners will agree on *one* picture they want to share with the class and mark it with a self-stick note.

Use *Airport* to model exploring a book and finding and marking a picture. Page through the book and think aloud about what you

Just the Facts — Unit 4 ▸ Week 1 ▸ Day 1

> **Teacher Note**
> You might say, "This picture shows what the inside of an airplane looks like, and it has labels that explain where the fuel tanks, cargo hold, and other parts of the plane are. That's interesting to me because I didn't know that the fuel tanks were in the wings. I'm going to mark it with a self-stick note so I can share that picture with the class later."

find interesting in one or two illustrations. Then choose and mark an illustration and explain why you think it is especially interesting.

6 ▸ Discuss Reaching Agreement About a Picture

Ask and briefly discuss:

Q *What will you and your partner do to decide which picture you want to share with the class?*

Q *If you don't agree at first, what can you do?*

> **Teacher Note**
> If the students have difficulty answering these questions, suggest some ideas like those in the "Students might say" note, and then ask for other ideas. If necessary, model finding a picture and reaching agreement with a student volunteer.

Students might say:

"I'll ask her what picture she likes and see if I like it, too."

"We'll talk until we find something we both like."

"If we don't agree on a picture, we can look for another one or ask you for help."

7 ▸ Explore Books in Pairs

Distribute a nonfiction book to each pair, showing each cover and reading each title aloud before handing it out. Remind the students that partners will look through their book together, talk about the pictures in it, and choose one picture that shows interesting information to share with the class. Give each pair a self-stick note to mark the picture they both like.

Give the students about 5 minutes to look at their books. Walk around and observe without intervening.

SHARING AND REFLECTING

8 ▸ Share Books and Reflect on Working With a New Partner

Invite each pair to share their book with the class. Ask them to show the cover and tell what the book is about. Then have them show the picture they marked and explain what they liked about it.

When all pairs have shared, ask and briefly discuss:

Q *What did you like about looking at a book with your partner?*

Q *What did you and your partner do to share the book fairly?*

Q *How did you and your partner agree on which picture to share with the class?*

Explain that tomorrow the students will continue to work with their partner and that they will have the chance to do some nonfiction writing.

◀ **Teacher Note**
Collect the nonfiction books and make them available for the students to read independently throughout the week.

EXTENSION

Write Facts About an Airport

Reread *Airport* aloud. Ask the students to choose one thing they learned about airports from the book and write and draw about it. Make the book available for the students to review as they write and draw, and encourage them to use words from the book in their writing. Have partners share their writing with each other. Then compile the writing in a class book called *Our Airport Book*.

Unit 4 ▶ Week 1

Day 2

Materials
- *Airport*
- Chart paper and a marker

Writing Nonfiction

In this lesson, the students:

- Generate a list of facts about the classroom
- Write a page for a class book about the classroom
- Get ideas by listening to others
- Take turns talking and listening

GETTING READY TO WRITE

 Briefly Review *Airport*

Gather the class with partners sitting together, facing you. Show the cover of *Airport* and remind the students that yesterday they heard and talked about the book. Ask and briefly discuss:

Q *What do you remember about the book* Airport*?*

If necessary, remind the students that *Airport* is a nonfiction book and that nonfiction books give facts, or true information, about something.

 Introduce Writing Facts About the Classroom

Remind the students that yesterday they learned about a special place—the airport. Explain that today the class will write a nonfiction book like *Airport* about another special place—their classroom.

Explain that each of them will write and draw a fact about the classroom; then you will collect the facts into a book to keep in the classroom library. Tell them that next year's kindergartners will be able to read the book and learn about the classroom.

272 | Being a Writer™

Unit 4 ▶ Week 1 ▶ Day 2   **Just the Facts**

 List Facts About the Classroom

Direct the students' attention to a sheet of chart paper entitled "Facts About Our Classroom." Explain that before they write a page for the class book, they will make a list of facts together as a class. Use "Think, Pair, Share" to have partners first think about and then discuss:

 Q *Look around the classroom. What interesting things do you see that we might tell about in our book?* [pause] *Turn to your partner.*

After a moment, signal for the students' attention and have a few volunteers share their ideas with the class. Write each fact as a sentence on the chart. (You might say, "[Jason] said that we have an aquarium with three fish, so I'll write the sentence, *We have an aquarium with three fish*.") As you write, point out that you are starting your sentences with a capital letter and ending them with a period.

Use "Think, Pair, Share" to have partners first think about and then discuss:

 Q *What interesting things do we do in our classroom?* [pause] *Turn to your partner.*

Signal for the students' attention. Have a few volunteers share their ideas and add the facts to the chart.

Facts About Our Classroom

We have an aquarium with three fish.

We have a mobile made out of cans.

We sing songs.

We write stories.

We count to 100.

Teacher Note

If the students have difficulty generating facts, stimulate their thinking by asking questions such as:

Q *What do you see on the [walls/tables/shelves] that we might tell about?*

◀ **Q** *What do you see in the corner? By the door?*

Q *What is something in our room that you especially like?*

◀ **Teacher Note**

In this unit you will continue to model and point out sentence punctuation for the students. While not all of the students are expected to consistently punctuate sentences correctly in their writing, some may do so.

◀ **Teacher Note**

If the students have difficulty generating facts, stimulate their thinking by asking questions such as:

Q *What do we do when we first come into our classroom? Then what do we do?*

Q *What do we do during [reading/writing/math] time?*

Q *What have we learned this year?*

Q *What special trips have we taken? What visitors have we had?*

Kindergarten | 273

ELL Note

You might number each fact on the chart so students can easily locate the fact they will write in their books in Step 4.

4 Choose Facts to Write and Draw About

Review that the students will each pick one fact about the classroom to write and draw about today. Point to the charted list and tell the students that they can write about one of the facts on the chart or any other fact they think of. Ask:

Q *What fact about our classroom will you write about? Turn and tell your partner.*

Distribute writing/drawing paper and have the students return to their seats.

WRITING TIME

Teacher Note

If you notice multiple students writing about the same fact, consider gently guiding them to choose different facts.

5 Write and Draw Facts About the Classroom

Have the students each write and draw a fact about the classroom. Encourage students who finish early to tell more by adding to their writing or drawing, or by writing another fact about the classroom on a new sheet of paper. As they work, walk around the room and observe.

> **CLASS ASSESSMENT NOTE**
>
> As you observe the students, ask yourself:
>
> - Are the students able to choose a fact and write and tell more about it?
> - Do they attempt to capitalize the first letters of sentences and use periods at the ends?
> - Do they write from left to right and leave spaces between words?
> - Do they approximate spelling by sounding out unfamiliar words?
>
> *continues*

Unit 4 ▶ Week 1 ▶ Day 2   **Just the Facts**

> **CLASS ASSESSMENT NOTE** *continued*
>
> Support struggling students by directing their attention to the "Facts About Our Classroom" chart and suggesting that they copy one of the facts. You might also ask them questions such as:
>
> **Q** *What do we do during [reading/writing/math] time? What can you draw to show that? What words might you write to tell about that?*
>
> **Q** *What special trips have we taken? What visitors have we had? What sentence can you write to tell about that?*

Signal to let the students know when writing time is over.

SHARING AND REFLECTING

 Reflect on Sharing

Gather the class with partners sitting together, facing you. Have the students bring their stories with them. Explain that partners will take turns sharing their writing with each other. Have partners turn to face each other and share their writing. As they share, observe pairs without intervening to see how well they are able to take turns talking and listening.

When most pairs have finished sharing, signal for the students' attention. Ask and discuss as a class:

Q *What new ideas did you get about our classroom from listening to your partner's story?*

Q *What did you do to make sure both you and your partner had a chance to share? What will you do [the same way/differently] next time so you both get to share?*

FACILITATION TIP

During this unit, we invite you to focus on **pacing class discussions** so they are lively and focused without dragging, losing participants, or wandering off the topic. Class discussions should be long enough to allow time for thinking and short enough to sustain attention. Good pacing requires careful observation of the class (not just the students who are responding) and the timely use of various pacing techniques.

To speed up a discussion:

- Call on just a few students to respond to each question, even if others have their hands up.

- Use "Turn to Your Partner" if many students want to speak; then call on just two or three students to share with the whole class.

To refocus or deepen a discussion:

- Restate the original question if the discussion goes off the topic.

- Ask pairs to discuss whether they agree or disagree with what a classmate has just said.

- Use wait-time before calling on anyone to respond.

Kindergarten | 275

Teacher Note

Save the "Facts About Our Classroom" chart to use on Day 3.

Students might say:

"I let my partner share first."

"I took turns talking with my partner."

"I made sure I only talked about my story."

Collect the students' papers for sharing on Day 3.

EXTENSION

Make a Labeled Drawing of the Classroom

Show the diagram on pages 12–13 of *Airport*. Explain that nonfiction writers often include pictures with labels in their books to give more information. Have the students add labels to their pictures to tell more about their classroom.

Unit 4 ▶ Week 1   Just the Facts

Day 3

Author's Chair Sharing

In this lesson, the students:

- Share their writing from the Author's Chair
- Use the prompts "I found out" and "I want to know"
- Act responsibly during Author's Chair sharing
- Discuss and solve problems that arise in their work together
- Write and draw freely

Materials
- Author's Chair
- "Facts About Our Classroom" chart from Day 2
- Students' writing from Day 2

GETTING READY TO SHARE

 Review Author's Chair Sharing

Gather the class with students sitting, facing the Author's Chair. Direct the students' attention to the "Facts About Our Classroom" chart. Remind the students that they made a list of facts about the classroom, and then each student chose a fact to write about for a class book about the classroom.

Explain that today the students will share their writing from the Author's Chair. Remind them that you will be sitting in the audience so they will be responsible for making sure Author's Chair sharing goes smoothly. Ask and briefly discuss:

Q *What can the author do to be responsible during Author's Chair sharing?*

Q *What can the audience do to be responsible during Author's Chair sharing?*

Students might say:

"The author should not start until it is quiet."

"The audience should look at the author."

"We can ask the author questions about his writing."

"The author should speak loudly and slowly."

Kindergarten | 277

Write the prompts *I found out* _____ and *I want to know* _____ where everyone can see them, and remind the students to use these prompts when they comment on one another's writing.

SHARING TIME

2 ▶ Share from the Author's Chair

Call on a student to share his writing from the Author's Chair. As you did in Unit 3, take your seat in the audience and have the student share. If necessary, remind the student to introduce himself as the author and illustrator, to show his illustration, and to read and tell about his writing in a loud, clear voice.

At the end of the sharing, lead the audience in clapping; then wait quietly until students begin to raise their hands to comment. If students do not raise their hands to comment after 15–20 seconds, raise your hand and comment on something you found out or something you want to know about the author's writing. If necessary, ask the class:

Q *What did you find out about our classroom from listening to [Ming's] writing?*

Q *What else do you want to know?*

Allow the author to call on two or three students who would like to comment on his writing. Follow this same procedure to have more students share from the Author's Chair. If there is not enough time for all of the students to share, tell them that the remaining students will share at another time.

Teacher Note

You might say, "I found out that our classroom [has a fish tank]" or "I want to know [who feeds the fish]."

Teacher Note

If necessary, plan more time for sharing so all of the students can share their stories from the Author's Chair.

REFLECTING

 Reflect on Sharing

Ask and briefly discuss:

Q *What did you do to be responsible during Author's Chair sharing today?*

> **Students might say:**
> "I looked at the author."
> "I didn't talk to my neighbor."
> "I asked [Zoe] if she could say her question again."

Q *What problems did you have with being responsible during Author's Chair sharing? What can you do next time to avoid those problems?*

Tell the students that next week they will hear another nonfiction book, do more writing, and share their writing with their classmates.

Teacher Note

Compile the students' writing into a class book and make a cover for it. Since the book will go into the class library, you might want to transcribe the students' words below their writing using conventional spelling and punctuation.

FREE WRITING TIME

 Write and Draw Freely

Give the students time to write and draw about anything they choose. They may write more nonfiction about a special place, or they may write about anything else. Tell the students to think quietly about what they might like to write and then have partners turn to each other and share their ideas.

Have a few volunteers share their ideas with the class; then distribute writing/drawing paper and have the students write and draw freely.

Teacher Note

If students have difficulty coming up with writing ideas, encourage them to look at the writing ideas charts from Unit 2.

Week 2 Overview

UNIT 4: JUST THE FACTS

Mr. Santizo's Tasty Treats!
by Alice K. Flanagan, photographs by Romie Flanagan
(Children's Press, 1998)

Mr. Santizo creates delicious treats at the neighborhood bakery.

Writing Focus

- Students hear and discuss a nonfiction book.
- Students interview their partner.
- Students write and draw a two-page book about their partner.
- Students write and punctuate sentences.

Social Focus

- Students work in a responsible way.
- Students listen respectfully to the thinking of others and share their own.
- Students express interest in and appreciation for one another's writing.
- Students act in fair and caring ways.

DO AHEAD

- Prior to Day 1, consider previewing this week's read-aloud, *Mr. Santizo's Tasty Treats!* with your English Language Learners. Read it aloud and show and discuss the pictures, or have the students flip through it on their own. (See page 283 for suggested ELL vocabulary.)

- Prior to Day 2, arrange for the principal, a teacher's aide, or another adult in the school to come to your class during writing time for an interview.

- Prior to Day 2, prepare two sheets of chart paper to look like the writing/drawing pages of the students' booklets (see the diagram on page 288). You will use one of these sheets on Day 2 and one on Day 3.

- Prior to Day 2, make a class set of two-page booklets by stapling together two sheets of writing/drawing paper for each student. (You will need a class set in Week 3 as well.)

TEACHER AS WRITER

"Curiosity urges you on—the driving force."
— *John Dos Passos*

Think of a colleague, friend, or family member you want to know more about and jot down questions you'd like to ask the person (for example, questions about the person's work and hobbies). Interview the person and write a brief profile.

You might ask questions such as:

- Who or what has been your biggest inspiration?
- How did you decide to become a [teacher]?
- What are your current goals or aspirations?
- If money were not an issue, what changes would you make in your daily life?

Unit 4 ▶ Week 2

Day 1

Exploring Nonfiction

Materials
- *Mr. Santizo's Tasty Treats!*
- *Airport* from Week 1
- Chart paper and a marker

In this lesson, the students:
- Hear and discuss a nonfiction book
- Generate a shared list of interesting people to write about
- Imagine and discuss how others might feel
- Write and draw freely

GETTING READY TO WRITE

 Introduce and Read *Mr. Santizo's Tasty Treats!* Aloud

Gather the class with partners sitting together, facing you. Show the cover of *Airport* and remind the students that last week they heard this book and began exploring nonfiction. Remind them that nonfiction books give true information (facts) about real things. Explain that this week the students will hear and discuss another nonfiction book and write a nonfiction book of their own.

Show the cover of *Mr. Santizo's Tasty Treats!* and tell the students that the nonfiction book they will hear today is about a real person named Mr. Santizo. Explain that Mr. Santizo is a *baker*, someone who *bakes*, or cooks food in the oven (such as breads, cakes, and cookies).

Read the title and the author's name aloud; then read the book aloud, showing the pictures and stopping as described on the next page. Clarify vocabulary as you read.

Suggested Vocabulary

Guatemala: country in Central America (p. 6)

orders: requests from people (p. 10)

ingredients: foods such as flour, milk, and eggs that are mixed together to make other foods (p. 11)

customers: people who buy things (p. 13)

frosts: puts frosting on (p. 18)

ELL Vocabulary

English Language Learners may benefit from discussing additional vocabulary, including:

treats: things that are fun to eat (p. 4)

trained: learned (p. 6)

recipe: list of directions for how to cook something (p. 14; see recipe on p. 31)

measures: makes sure he has the right amount of (p. 15)

decorated: covered with sprinkles, flowers, and writing that make it look special (p. 19)

Stop after:

p. 7 "Now the Santizos have three children. They are very proud of them."

Ask:

Q *What have you learned about Mr. Santizo so far?*

Have a few volunteers share their answers. As they share, show the corresponding pages in the book.

Students might say:

"Mr. Santizo is a baker."

"He used to wash dishes for his job."

"Mr. Santizo has three children."

Reread the sentence on page 7 and continue reading. Follow the same procedure at the next stopping point:

p. 17 "…the sharp knives, and the hot ovens."

Reread the last sentence on pages 16–17 and continue reading to the end of the book.

◀ **Teacher Note**

If the students have trouble recalling what they heard, reread pages 3–7.

2 Briefly Discuss the Reading

Ask and briefly discuss:

Q *What's interesting about Mr. Santizo?*

Point out that the author, Alice K. Flanagan, has written several nonfiction books about other interesting people that work in the community. Explain that she writes books about people like Mr. Santizo so that we can learn about their work and get to know them better.

SHARED WRITING

3 Generate Ideas for People to Learn and Write About

On a sheet of chart paper, write the title "People in Our School Community." Read the title aloud and explain that together the students will make a list of interesting people in their school that they might want to learn and write about. Interesting people might include other teachers, the librarian, lunchroom workers, and parent volunteers. Use "Think, Pair, Share" to have partners first think about and then discuss:

 Q *What people at our school might you like to learn and write about?* [pause] *Turn to your partner.*

Signal for the students' attention and have a few volunteers share their ideas with the class. As they share, record their ideas on the chart. If necessary, prompt them to give more information about each person by asking questions such as:

Q *What does [Mrs. Agnew] do at our school?*

Teacher Note

If the students have difficulty thinking of people in the school community, prompt them by asking questions such as:

Q *Who are other teachers you know in the school?*

Q *What other adults help you?*

Q *Who do you see in the office? Playground? Lunchroom?*

Q *Who helps us in our classroom?*

If the name of the person you have arranged to interview on Day 2 does not appear on the chart, be sure to add it. (You might say, "I would really like to learn more about our principal, [Mr. Perkins]. I'm going to add his name to our chart.")

REFLECTING

4 Discuss Acting in Caring Ways

Tell the students that you will invite one of the interesting people on the chart to visit the class during writing time tomorrow. Explain that they will learn about the person and then use that information to write a shared nonfiction book about him or her. Ask and briefly discuss:

Q *What will we do tomorrow to treat our guest in a caring way?*

Q *How do you think our guest will feel if we treat [him/her] in a caring way? Why do we want our guests to feel that way?*

> **Students might say:**
>
> "We can say 'good morning' to our guest."
>
> "We can be good listeners."
>
> "I think it will make our guest feel happy."
>
> "We want our guests to feel happy so they will come back and visit us again."

Encourage the students to keep these ideas in mind when the guest is in the classroom tomorrow, and explain that you will check in with them tomorrow to see how they did.

FREE WRITING TIME

5 Write and Draw Freely

Give the students time to write and draw about anything they choose. Tell the students to think quietly about what they might like to write and then have partners turn to each other and share their ideas.

Have a few volunteers share their ideas with the class; then distribute writing/drawing paper and have the students write and draw freely.

Just the Facts

FACILITATION TIP

Continue to focus on **pacing class discussions** so they are neither too short nor too long. Scan the whole class (not just the students who are responding) and use techniques such as the following:

- Call on just a few students to respond to each question, even if others have their hands up.
- Use "Turn to Your Partner" if many students want to speak; then call on just two or three students to share with the whole class.
- Restate the original question if the discussion goes off the topic.
- Ask pairs to discuss whether they agree or disagree with what a classmate has just said.
- Use wait-time before calling on anyone to respond.

◀ **Teacher Note**

You might want to review this discussion with your students tomorrow, right before the lesson.

Teacher Note

If the students have difficulty coming up with writing ideas, encourage them to look at the charts of writing ideas from Unit 2.

Teacher Note

Save the "People in Our School Community" chart to use on Day 2.

Kindergarten | 285

EXTENSION

Read More Books by Alice Flanagan

The students may enjoy reading more books about people in the community by Alice K. Flanagan, including *Buying a Pet from Ms. Chavez*, *Choosing Eyeglasses with Mrs. Koutris*, *Learning Is Fun with Mrs. Perez*, and *Mr. Yee Fixes Cars*.

Day 2

Writing Nonfiction

In this lesson, the students:

- Observe an interview with an interesting person
- Interview and write about their partner
- Act considerately toward others
- Work responsibly in pairs
- Thank one another for their help

GETTING READY TO WRITE

1 Introduce the Guest

Gather the class with partners sitting together, facing you. Show the cover of *Mr. Santizo's Tasty Treats!* and remind the students that yesterday they learned about an interesting person from this book. Direct the students' attention to the "People in Our School Community" chart and review that they created a list of interesting people in the school that they wanted to learn more about.

Remind the students that you have invited one of the people on the list to be a guest in the classroom today. Point to the person's name on the chart and then introduce the guest. Lead the students in welcoming the guest and thanking him for coming (for example, "This is [Mr. Perkins], our principal. Let's welcome him by saying, 'Good morning, [Mr. Perkins]. Thank you for coming'").

 Interview the Guest

Explain that to find out more about your guest so you can write about him, you will *interview* him, or ask him questions. Ask the students to watch as you interview the guest.

Materials

- *Mr. Santizo's Tasty Treats!*
- "People in Our School Community" chart from Day 1
- Adult for modeling interviewing (see "Do Ahead" on page 281)
- Sample book page chart for modeling (see "Do Ahead" on page 281) and a marker
- Class set of two-page booklets (see "Do Ahead" on page 281)

Ask your guest the following questions and have the guest respond.

Q *[Mr. Perkins], what is your favorite thing to do outdoors?*

Q *[Mr. Perkins], what is your favorite thing to do indoors?*

Ask the class:

Q *What other questions would you like to ask [Mr. Perkins]?*

Give your guest an opportunity to respond to several questions from the class; then ask the class:

Q *What have you learned about [Mr. Perkins]?*

3 Model Writing a Page About the Guest

Direct the students' attention to the sample book page you prepared. Ask them to watch as you write the first page of a nonfiction book about the guest. Explain that the first page will be about what the guest does for fun outside. Ask the guest to help you spell his name. Write the rest of the sentence, pointing out that you are starting your sentence with a capital letter and ending it with a period.

Teacher Note

You might say, "[Mr. Perkins] said that he hikes in the hills with his dog, so I'll write *Mr. Perkins hikes in the hills with his dog*. [Mr. Perkins], could you please spell your name for me? Thank you for your help. I need to make sure the first letter of the sentence is a capital letter, and that I put a period at the end. I'll draw a picture of [Mr. Perkins] and his dog, with some trees around him."

When you have finished writing, have the class thank the guest for visiting today and say goodbye.

WRITING TIME

 Have Partners Interview Each Other

Tell the students that they will now follow your model and interview and write about another interesting person, their partner. Show a sample two-page booklet and explain that they will write a book about their partner using such a booklet. Point to the first page, explaining that they will write the first page today and they will continue writing on the second page tomorrow.

Have the students move to desks with partners sitting together. Explain that partners will ask each other the question, "What is your favorite thing to do outdoors?" They will then write what their partner says on the first page of their booklet.

Have partners begin interviewing each other. As they talk, distribute a two-page booklet to each student. When most pairs have finished talking, signal for the students' attention.

Direct the students' attention to your charted sample book page and reread your sentence aloud. Explain that you would like the students to follow your example and begin their own sentence with their partner's name. Ask:

Q *What sentence will you write about your partner's favorite thing to do outdoors?*

Have a few volunteers share their thinking with the class.

> **Students might say:**
>
> "I'll write *Marcus flies his kite at the park.*"
>
> "I'll write *Cam plays baseball.*"
>
> "I'll write *Danita jumps rope at recess.*"

◀ **Teacher Note**

Listen as partners interview each other. If the students are struggling to ask or answer the question, call for their attention and invite a pair of students to model asking each other the question.

 Write About Their Partner

Have the students each write and draw their partner's favorite thing to do outdoors on the first page of their booklet. Encourage partners to help each other spell their names. Have students who finish early tell more about their partner by adding to their writing or drawing.

Teacher Note

Save your charted sample book page to use on Day 3.

As the pairs work, walk around and observe.

Signal to let the students know when writing time is over. Collect the students' booklets (keeping partners' booklets together). Explain that tomorrow partners will interview each other again and write the second page of their books.

REFLECTING

 Reflect on Acting in Caring Ways

Ask and briefly discuss:

Q *What did we do to treat [our guest/each other] in caring ways today?*

Q *What did you and your partner do to help each other?*

Students might say:

"We said 'good morning' to [Mr. Perkins]."

"We looked at [Mr. Perkins] while he was talking."

"We thanked him for coming to our classroom."

"I listened to my partner."

"My partner helped me spell his name."

Have partners thank each other for helping and for acting in caring ways.

Unit 4 ▶ Week 2

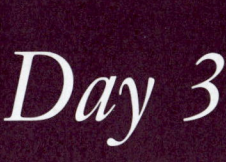

Day 3

Writing Nonfiction and Sharing

In this lesson, the students:

- Interview and write about their partner
- Work responsibly in pairs
- Share their writing in pairs from the Authors' Chairs
- Use the prompts "I found out" and "I want to know"
- Thank one another for their help

GETTING READY TO WRITE

 Model Writing a Second Page About Yesterday's Guest

Gather the class with partners sitting together, facing you. Briefly review that the students interviewed and wrote the first page of a nonfiction book about an interesting person, their partner. Explain that today they are going to write the second page of their book.

Remind the students that yesterday they helped you interview and write about an interesting person who visited the class. Direct the students' attention to the sample book page from Day 2 and read it aloud. Ask:

Q *What else did we learn about [Mr. Perkins]?*

Q *What was [Mr. Perkins'] favorite thing to do indoors?*

Ask the students to watch as you model writing the second page of your book about the guest. On the second sample book page, write and illustrate a sentence about the guest's favorite thing to do indoors. As you write, point out that you are starting your sentence with a capital letter and ending it with a period.

Just the Facts

Materials

- Sample book page from Day 2
- Second sample book page chart for modeling (see "Do Ahead" on page 281) and a marker
- Students' booklets from Day 2
- Two chairs for Author's Chair sharing

◀ **Teacher Note**

Be ready to remind the students of how your guest answered the questions from Day 2.

◀ **Teacher Note**

You might say, "[Mr. Perkins] said that he plays the guitar, so I'll write *Mr. Perkins plays the guitar*. Notice that the first word of the sentence begins with a capital letter and that I put a period at the end of the sentence. I'll draw a picture of [Mr. Perkins] with his guitar."

Kindergarten | 291

Just the Facts Unit 4 ▶ Week 2 ▶ Day 3

WRITING TIME

2 ▶ **Have Partners Interview Each Other**

Tell the students that they will interview their partner again and write a second page about him or her in their booklets.

Have the students return to their seats with partners sitting together. Explain that partners will ask each other the question, "What is your favorite thing to do indoors?" They will then write what their partner says on the second page of their booklet.

Have partners interview each other. As they talk, return the students' booklets to them. When most pairs have finished talking, signal for their attention.

Direct the students' attention to today's charted sample book page and reread your sentence aloud. Explain that you would like the students to do as they did yesterday and begin today's sentence with their partner's name. Ask:

Q *What sentence will you write about your partner's favorite thing to do indoors?*

Teacher Note ▶

As you did on Day 2, listen as partners interview each other. If the students struggle to ask or answer the question, invite a pair of students to model asking each other the question while the other students watch.

Have a few volunteers share their thinking with the class.

> ***Students might say:***
>
> "I'll write *Marcus builds with the blocks.*"
>
> "I'll write *Cam plays with puzzles.*"
>
> "I'll write *Danita reads her picture books.*"

 Write About Their Partner

Have the students write and draw their partner's favorite thing to do indoors on the second page of their booklets. Encourage partners to help each other spell their names again, if necessary. Have students who finish early tell more about their partner by adding to their writing or drawing.

As the pairs work, walk around and observe.

CLASS ASSESSMENT NOTE

As you observe the students, ask yourself:

- Do the students write, or attempt to write, sentences?
- Do their illustrations match what they wrote?
- Do they attempt to capitalize the first letters of sentences and use periods at the ends?
- Do they sound out words and use the word wall?
- Do they tell more in their writing by adding to their writing or drawing?

Support struggling students by paging through *Mr. Santizo's Tasty Treats!* with them, pointing out how the pictures match the words. Also point out spaces between words, capitalization, and punctuation.

Signal to let the students know when writing time is over.

SHARING AND REFLECTING

4▶ Share Books from the Authors' Chairs

Gather the class with partners sitting together, facing the Authors' Chairs. Have them bring their story booklets with them. Explain that partners will share the books they wrote about each other from the Authors' Chairs.

Write the prompts *I found out* _____ and *I want to know* _____ where everyone can see them, and remind students to use these prompts when they comment on their classmates' writing.

Call on a pair to sit in the Authors' Chairs and take turns reading and telling about their books. Take your seat in the audience and have the students share. After each pair shares, lead the audience in clapping; then wait quietly until students begin to raise their hands to comment. If students do not raise their hands to comment after 15–20 seconds, raise your hand and comment on something you found out or something you want to know about the authors' writing. If necessary, ask the class:

Q *What did you find out about [Manny] from [Bari's] book?*

Q *What more do you want to know about [Manny] and [Bari]?*

Allow the authors to call on two or three students who would like to comment on their books. Follow this same procedure to have more pairs share from the Authors' Chairs. If there is not enough time for all of the pairs to share, tell them that the remaining pairs will share at another time.

5▶ Reflect on Sharing

Ask and briefly discuss:

Q *What did you do to act in caring ways during sharing time?*

Q *What caring things did you notice other people doing?*

Have partners thank each other for helping and for acting in caring ways.

Teacher Note

You may prefer to have the students share their books at another time later in the day or week. You might invite another class or parents to attend a reading of the books. If you choose to share at another time, collect the students' booklets and explain that they will share their books later in the day or week.

Teacher Note

If necessary, plan more time for sharing so all of the pairs can share their writing from the Authors' Chairs.

EXTENSION

Have the Students Make Covers for Their Books

Show the covers of *Airport* and *Mr. Santizo's Tasty Treats!* and ask the students what they notice about the covers. Explain that a book cover usually has these three parts: a title that tells what the book is about, the name of the author, and an illustration that shows something about the book. Have partners discuss what titles they might give their books and what pictures they might draw on the covers. Then have the students make covers using construction paper or cardstock. Consider placing the students' books in the class library for others to read and enjoy.

Week 3 Overview

UNIT 4: JUST THE FACTS

I Like Pasta
by Jennifer Julius
(Children's Press, 2001)

Spaghetti, macaroni, ravioli…many varieties of pasta are described.

Writing Focus

- Students hear and discuss a nonfiction book.
- Students use their senses to generate facts about a food.
- Students write and draw a two-page book about a food.
- Students write and punctuate sentences.

Social Focus

- Students work in a responsible way.
- Students listen respectfully to the thinking of others and share their own.
- Students express interest in and appreciation for one another's writing.

DO AHEAD

- Prior to Day 1, consider previewing this week's read-aloud, *I Like Pasta*, with your English Language Learners. Read it aloud and show and discuss the pictures, or have the students flip through it on their own.
- Prior to Day 2, bring in enough grapes so that each student has a small bunch to examine plus some extras to eat before or after the lesson.
- Prior to Day 2, prepare a sheet of chart paper so that it looks like one of the writing/drawing pages of the students' booklets (see the diagram on page 303).
- Prior to Day 2, make a class set of two-page booklets by stapling together two sheets of writing/drawing paper for each student.
- Prior to Day 3, bring in enough raisins so that each student has a few to examine plus some extras to eat before or after the lesson.

TEACHER AS WRITER

"Being a nonfiction writer means that I can explore any subject that interests me."
— Russell Freedman

This week, create a list of nonfiction subjects that interest you. Choose one subject from your list to explore. See what you can find out about that topic this week and jot down any new facts you learn. Organize the facts in a way that makes sense, thinking about:

- What is the best order to organize the information?
- How might I make the information easy to understand?
- How might I present the information in an interesting way?

Unit 4 ▶ Week 3

Day 1

Materials

- *I Like Pasta*
- *Airport* from Week 1
- *Mr. Santizo's Tasty Treats!* from Week 2
- Chart paper and a marker

Exploring Nonfiction

In this lesson, the students:

- Hear and discuss a nonfiction book
- Explore a table of contents
- Generate ideas about foods to write about
- Share their partner's thinking with the class
- Write and draw freely

GETTING READY TO WRITE

 Introduce and Read Part of *I Like Pasta* Aloud

Gather the class with partners sitting together, facing you. Show the books *Airport* and *Mr. Santizo's Tasty Treats!* and remind the students that over the past two weeks they heard and talked about these nonfiction books and wrote nonfiction. Explain that this week they will hear a new nonfiction book and write another nonfiction book of their own.

Show the cover of *I Like Pasta* and read the title and the name of the author aloud. Tell the students that the nonfiction book they will hear today is about a kind of food called *pasta*. Point to the dish of spaghetti on the cover and explain that spaghetti noodles and foods like it are called pasta.

Open the book to the table of contents (page 3), and point to and read the word "Contents" aloud. Explain that some nonfiction books have a page like this that tells what information is in the book and the pages where you can find the information. Explain that today you will read the first three parts of the book, and that each part tells about a dish made with pasta. Point to and read the first three chapter titles aloud ("Spaghetti," "Ravioli," and "Lasagna").

Turn to page 6 and read the first chapter, "Spaghetti," aloud, showing the picture on page 7. Stop reading at the end of page 6 and ask:

 Q *What did you find out about [spaghetti]? Turn to your partner.*

Have a few volunteers share their answers. As they share, reread the corresponding sentences to the class.

Follow the same procedure to have the students hear and discuss the chapter about ravioli (pages 8–9) and lasagna (pages 10–11). Remind the students to listen carefully for facts as you read.

Point out that the author, Jennifer Julius, has written several nonfiction books about different foods. Explain that she writes books like *I Like Pasta* to help us learn about foods many people like to eat.

SHARED WRITING

 Generate Ideas for Foods to Learn and Write About

On a sheet of chart paper, write the title "Foods We Can Write About." Read the title aloud and explain that together you will make a list of foods that the students like to eat and might want to learn and write about. Use "Think, Pair, Share" to have partners first think about and then discuss the question that follows. Alert the students to listen carefully, as they will share their partner's thinking with the class.

 Q *What foods would you like to learn and write about?* [pause] *Turn to your partner.*

Signal for the students' attention and have a few volunteers share what their partner said with the class. As they share, record their ideas on the chart.

Teacher Note

Encourage the students to think of fruits and vegetables they like, in addition to other foods. If *grapes* does not appear on the chart, be sure to add it in preparation for the Day 2 lesson. (You might say, "I would really like to learn more about grapes. I'm going to add *grapes* to our chart.")

REFLECTING

 Reflect on Sharing Their Partner's Thinking

Ask and briefly discuss:

Q *What did you do to make sure you could share what your partner said with the class?*

Q *If you weren't sure what your partner said, what can you do next time so you can share your partner's thinking with the class?*

Explain that tomorrow the students will learn more about one of the foods on the chart by observing it, or looking at it carefully. Then they will use that information to write a nonfiction book about it.

Teacher Note

Make *I Like Pasta* available so that interested students can read the rest of it on their own.

Teacher Note

Save the "Foods We Can Write About" chart to use on Day 2.

FREE WRITING TIME

 Write and Draw Freely

Give the students time to write and draw about anything they choose. Tell the students to think quietly about what they might like to write and then have partners turn to each other and share their ideas.

Have a few volunteers share their ideas with the class; then distribute writing/drawing paper and have the students write and draw freely.

EXTENSION

Introduce the Glossary in *I Like Pasta*

Show the glossary in *I Like Pasta* (page 22) and point to and read the words "New Words." Explain that some nonfiction books have a page like this that lists words readers might not know. Tell the students that next to each word, the author has shown how to say the word, and has explained what the word means. Read the words and definitions aloud.

Day 2

Unit 4 ▶ Week 3

Just the Facts

Writing Nonfiction

In this lesson, the students:

- Make observations and generate facts about grapes
- Write about grapes
- Handle materials responsibly

GETTING READY TO WRITE

1 **Briefly Review and Introduce Grapes**

Have partners sit together at desks today. Show the cover of *I Like Pasta*, and remind the students that yesterday they heard and talked about part of the book. Review the "Foods We Can Write About" chart, reminding the students that they listed foods that they wanted to learn and write about. Tell students that today they will learn and write about one of these foods.

Hold up a bunch of grapes. Ask and briefly discuss:

Q *What do you know about grapes?*

Explain that grapes are a fruit that grow in bunches on vines (plants with long, thin stems). Tell the students that they will each receive a small bunch of grapes to look at closely; then they will write the first page of a nonfiction book about grapes.

2 **Discuss Handling Grapes Responsibly**

Ask and briefly discuss:

Q *What will you do to be responsible when you receive your grapes?*

Materials

- *I Like Pasta*
- "Foods We Can Write About" chart from Day 1
- Small bunch of grapes (3–4 grapes) for each student, plus some extras to eat (see "Do Ahead" on page 297)
- Chart paper and a marker
- Sample book page chart for modeling (see "Do Ahead" on page 297)
- Class set of two-page booklets (see "Do Ahead" on page 297)

Kindergarten | 301

Just the Facts   Unit 4 ▸ Week 3 ▸ Day 2

Students might say:

"We can keep the grapes on our tables."

"We can pick them up if they drop on the floor."

"I will keep my hands on my own grapes and not touch anyone else's."

Encourage the students to keep these ideas in mind during the lesson and explain that you will check in with them later to see how they did.

3 ▸ Generate Facts About Grapes

Give each student a small bunch of grapes. Explain that you will ask them some questions to help them think of some facts about the grapes. Ask each of the following questions, one at a time (without discussing them), pausing between each question to give the students time to observe and think.

Q *What do the grapes look like?*

Q *What color are they?*

Q *What shape are they?*

Q *What do the grapes feel like?*

Q *What else do you notice about the grapes?*

Have partners turn and talk to each other about their observations.

Signal for the students' attention and have a few volunteers share their observations with the class. As they share, write their observations as short sentences on a sheet of chart paper entitled "Things We Observe About Grapes."

Teacher Note

If students want to eat the grapes, you might want to give them a few to eat separately, before they examine the grape bunches for their writing.

Teacher Note

Listen as partners share. If the students have difficulty describing what a grape looks or feels like, call for their attention and ask them to look again at the grape. Repeat the questions, stopping after each one to discuss what the students notice. You might model gently rubbing or squeezing the grape and asking the following questions:

Q *Gently rub the skin of the grape with your fingers. How does the skin feel?*

Q *Gently squeeze the grape with your fingers. How does that feel?*

Things We Observe About Grapes

Grapes are purple.
Grapes are round.
They have stems.
They grow in a bunch.
They are smooth.
They are squishy.

4 ▶ Model Writing a Page About Grapes

Direct the students' attention to the chart of a sample book page you prepared. Ask them to watch as you write the first page of a nonfiction book about grapes. Pick a few sentences from the "Things We Observe About Grapes" chart (for example, *Grapes are round. They have stems and they grow in a bunch*). Write the sentences on your sample book page. Do a quick sketch showing what your bunch of grapes looks like.

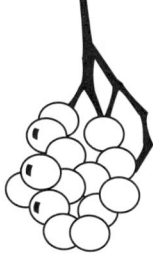

Grapes are round. They have stems and they grow in a bunch.

WRITING TIME

 Write About Grapes

Tell the students that they will write their own page about grapes using sentences from the class chart or other sentences about their observations. Show a sample two-page booklet and explain that they will write on the first page today and they will continue writing on the second page tomorrow.

Distribute a two-page booklet to each student and have them write the first page of their book about grapes. As they work, walk around and observe.

Signal to let the students know when writing time is over. Collect the students' booklets and tell them that they will write the second page of their book about grapes tomorrow.

REFLECTING

 Reflect on Working in a Responsible Way

Ask and briefly discuss:

Q *What did you do to be responsible while you were working with your grapes today?*

Q *What problems did we have with handling the grapes responsibly? What can we do next time to be more responsible?*

EXTENSION

Practice the Skill of Observation

Introduce the poem "The Little Turtle" by Vachel Lindsay (*Read-Aloud Rhymes for the Very Young*, page 20). Explain that in order to write this poem the poet had to watch the turtle very carefully. Tell the students that, as you read "The Little Turtle" aloud, you want them to listen for facts or true information about the turtle. Read the poem aloud slowly and clearly. Ask and briefly discuss:

Q *What did you find out about the turtle?*

Provide an opportunity for students to observe an animal (such as a class pet) or objects (such as rocks or shells) and write about what they see. Compile the pages into a class book entitled *Things We Observe*.

Unit 4 ▶ Week 3

Writing Nonfiction and Sharing

In this lesson, the students:

- Make observations and generate facts about raisins
- Write about raisins
- Handle materials responsibly
- Share writing in pairs

GETTING READY TO WRITE

1 **Introduce Raisins**

Have partners sit together at desks today. Briefly review that the students observed grapes and wrote the first page of a nonfiction book about grapes yesterday. Explain that today, they are going to write the second page of their book.

Hold up a raisin (or a box of raisins). Ask and briefly discuss:

Q *What do you know about raisins?*

Explain that raisins are grapes that have been dried. Tell the students that they will receive a few raisins to look at closely; then they will write about raisins on the second page of their nonfiction book. Ask and briefly discuss:

Q *What will you do to be responsible while you are observing the raisins today?*

Encourage the students to keep these ideas in mind during the lesson, and explain that you will check in with them later to see how they did.

Materials

- 3–4 raisins for each student, plus some extras to eat (see "Do Ahead" on page 297)
- Chart paper and a marker
- Students' booklets from Day 2

FACILITATION TIP

Reflect on your experience over the past three weeks with **pacing class discussions**. Do the pacing techniques feel comfortable and natural for you? Do you find yourself using them throughout the school day? What effect has your focus on pacing had on your students' participation in discussions? We encourage you to continue to think about how to pace class discussions throughout the year.

306 | Being a Writer™

Generate Facts About Raisins

Give each student a few raisins. Explain that you will ask some questions to help the students think of some facts about the raisins. Ask each of the following questions, one at a time (without discussing them), pausing between each question to give the students time to observe and think.

Q *What do raisins look like?*

Q *Are they bigger or smaller than grapes?*

Q *What color are they?*

Q *What shape are they?*

Q *What do raisins feel like?*

Have partners turn and talk to each other about their observations.

Signal for the students' attention and have a few volunteers share their observations with the class. As they share, write their observations as short sentences on a sheet of chart paper entitled "Things We Observe About Raisins."

Things We Observe About Raisins

Raisins are bumpy.

Raisins are dark purple.

They are rough.

They are sticky.

They are smaller than grapes.

◀ **Teacher Note**

If students want to eat their raisins, you might give them a few to eat before they examine raisins for their writing.

◀ **Teacher Note**

As you did yesterday, listen as partners share. If the students have difficulty describing what raisins are like, call for their attention and repeat the questions, stopping after each one to discuss what the students notice. If the students continue to struggle, suggest some ideas like those in the diagram.

WRITING TIME

 Write About Raisins

Tell the students that they will write about raisins on the second page of their grape book. They may use a sentence from the class chart or another sentence about their observations. Return the students' booklets to them and have them write the second page of their books. As they work, walk around and observe.

> **CLASS ASSESSMENT NOTE**
>
> As you observe the students, ask yourself:
>
> - Do the students write, or attempt to write, sentences?
> - Do their illustrations match what they wrote?
> - Do they attempt to capitalize the first letters of sentences and use periods at the ends?
> - Do they sound out words and use the word wall?
> - Do they tell more in their writing by adding to their writing or drawing?
>
> Support struggling students by paging through *I Like Pasta* with them, pointing out how the pictures match the words. Also point out spaces between words, capitalization, and punctuation.

Signal to let the students know when writing time is over.

SHARING AND REFLECTING

 Share Books in Pairs

Gather the class with partners sitting together, facing you. Have the students bring their story booklets with them. Explain that partners will share the books they wrote about grapes and raisins with each other. Alert them to listen carefully, as they will share something their partner wrote with the class.

Have partners share their books with each other. When most pairs have finished sharing, signal for the students' attention and ask:

Q *What did you find out about grapes from your partner's book?*

Have a few volunteers share what their partner wrote with the class. Encourage them to use the prompt "I found out" to share their thinking with the class.

Remind the students that one reason authors write nonfiction books is to help readers learn about something. Encourage the students to take their books home and share them with their families so they, too, can learn interesting facts about grapes.

5 Reflect on Working in a Responsible Way

Ask and briefly discuss:

Q *What did you do to be responsible while you were observing your raisin today?*

Q *What did you do to be a responsible partner?*

Have a few volunteers share their thinking with the class. Have partners take a moment to thank each other for their work together in this unit.

Teacher Note

This is the last week in Unit 4. You will need to reassign partners before starting Unit 5.

EXTENSIONS

Write Additional Pages for the Book About Grapes

Have the students each eat a grape and discuss what they notice about the taste and how it feels in their mouth. Then have them each write a third page for their book to describe how a grape tastes. Follow the same procedure to add another page about raisins.

Have the Students Make Covers for Their Books

Show the cover of *I Like Pasta* and review that a cover has three parts: a title that tells what the book is about, the name of the author, and an illustration that shows something about the book. Have partners discuss what titles they might give their books and what pictures they might draw on the covers. Then have the students make book covers using construction paper or cardstock.

Unit 5

Exploring Words Through Poetry

Unit 5

Exploring Words Through Poetry

During this three-week unit, the students explore words through hearing, discussing, and writing poems. They act out and visualize to make sense of poems and to get ideas for their own poems. They explore interesting words they hear in poems and generate lists of interesting words to use in their own poems. They share their poems in pairs and as a class and create individual books of poetry. They review approximating spelling and using the word wall. Socially, they build on one another's thinking and learn to use the prompt "I imagined" to express interest in one another's poems.

UNIT OVERVIEW

WEEK	DAY 1	DAY 2	DAY 3
1	**Exploring Poems:** "Wide Awake," "Shore," "Blowing Bubbles" **Focus:** • Acting out and visualizing poems • Writing and drawing freely	**Exploring Poems and Words:** "Toaster Time," "The Frog on the Log" **Focus:** • Visualizing poems • Exploring interesting words in a poem • Writing and drawing freely	**Exploring Poems:** "Chums" **Focus:** • Visualizing poems • Drawing visualizations • Sharing drawings
2	**Exploring Poems and Words:** "Mice" **Focus:** • Exploring descriptive words • Generating descriptive words about animals • Contributing to a shared poem • Writing and drawing freely	**Writing Poems:** "Fish" **Focus:** • Exploring movement words • Generating movement words about animals • Writing poems about animals • Sharing favorite words	**Writing Poems:** "The Squirrel" **Focus:** • Exploring descriptive words • Writing poems about animals • Sharing favorite words
3	**Exploring Poems and Words:** "The Meal," "Crunch and Lick" **Focus:** • Exploring descriptive words • Generating descriptive words about foods • Contributing to a shared poem • Writing and drawing freely	**Writing Poems:** "Yellow Butter" **Focus:** • Exploring color words in a poem • Writing poems about foods • Sharing favorite words	**Author's Chair Sharing** **Focus:** • Sharing poems from the Author's Chair • Learning the prompt "I imagined" • Writing and drawing freely

Kindergarten | 313

Week 1 Overview

UNIT 5: EXPLORING WORDS THROUGH POETRY

Read-Aloud Rhymes for the Very Young
selected by Jack Prelutsky, illustrated by Marc Brown
(Alfred A. Knopf, 1986)

Animals, bugs, and other topics are all presented in rhyme.

Unit 5 ▸ Week 1 — Exploring Words Through Poetry

Writing Focus

- Students hear, discuss, and act out poems.
- Students visualize to make sense of poems.
- Students draw and write about their visualizations.

Social Focus

- Students work in a responsible way.
- Students make decisions and solve problems respectfully.

DO AHEAD

- Prior to Day 1, decide how you will randomly assign partners to work together during this unit. See the front matter in volume 1 for suggestions about assigning partners randomly (page xiii) and considerations for pairing English Language Learners (page xxvi).

- Prior to Day 1, review some of the nursery rhymes, chants, songs, and poems the students have learned this year. If your students have not heard much poetry this year, consider taking time to immerse them in poems before you proceed with this unit. Read poems aloud, act them out, and move and clap to their rhythms. To find poems online, search using the keywords "children's poems."

- Preread this week's poems with your English Language Learners. If possible, show them related illustrations, photographs, or objects (such as soapy water and wands for the poem "Blowing Bubbles" or a toaster for the poem "Toaster Time") to aid their comprehension.

- Prior to Day 2, copy the poem "Toaster Time" from *Read-Aloud Rhymes for the Very Young* (page 50) onto chart paper.

- Prior to Day 3, copy the poem "Chums" from *Read-Aloud Rhymes for the Very Young* (page 40) onto chart paper.

TEACHER AS WRITER

"Poetry is language at its most distilled and most powerful."
— Rita Dove

This week, seek out poems that inspire you. Websites offering wide selections of poems include the Academy of American Poets website (www.poets.org), *Poetry* magazine's website (www.poetryfoundation.org), and Poetry Daily (www.poems.com). You might also search online using the keyword "poems."

Keep in mind that it is not necessary to completely understand a poem in order to appreciate something about it. Choose a few poems you especially enjoy and copy or paste them into your writing notebook. Jot down what you like about them—word choices, figurative language (such as similes, metaphors, and personification), the length or shape of the poems, or anything else you notice.

Day 1

Unit 5 ▶ Week 1

Materials

- "Wide Awake," "Shore," and "Blowing Bubbles" (*Read-Aloud Rhymes for the Very Young*, pages 82, 30, and 9)

Exploring Poems

In this lesson, the students:

- Work with a new partner
- Hear, visualize, and act out poems
- Move around the room responsibly
- Work responsibly in pairs
- Write and draw freely

About Writing Poems in Kindergarten

Hearing poems gives young writers the opportunity to savor and discuss words. The primary focus of this unit is to expand the students' writing vocabularies by introducing them to the vivid language of poems. During the unit, the students discuss interesting words they hear in poems, generate lists of interesting words, and use those words to write poems. The students explore elements of poetry such as rhyme, rhythm, and repetition, preparing them for a more formal study of these elements in later grades.

As you read aloud and discuss poems, write shared poems, and support your students' writing, adopt a relaxed attitude and keep the focus on having fun with words. Also, listen carefully to your students during discussions and the writing of shared poems; children have a natural affinity for the inventive, musical language of poetry.

GETTING READY TO READ

 Meet New Partners

Randomly assign partners (see "Do Ahead" on page 315). Gather the class with partners sitting together, facing you. Give new partners a moment to chat informally and get to know each other.

Signal for the students' attention and explain that during the next few weeks partners will share their thinking and writing with each other. Ask and briefly discuss:

Q *What will you do to work responsibly with your partner?*

Making Meaning® Teacher

You can either have the students work with their *Making Meaning* partner or assign a different partner for the writing lessons.

Q *Why is it important that you and your partner work responsibly together?*

Students might say:

"We can share our ideas."

"We can listen and not be silly."

"It's important so we can help each other with our writing."

"We can both learn better."

Tell the students that you will check in with them during the week to see how they are doing working responsibly with their partner.

READING TIME

 Read, Visualize, and Act Out "Wide Awake"

Remind the students that they have heard and written many stories this year. Explain that during the next few weeks they will explore another kind of writing—poems. Briefly mention some of the nursery rhymes, chants, and other poems they have heard this year.

Ask the students to close their eyes and make a picture in their minds as they listen to a poem. Read "Wide Awake" by Myra Cohn Livingston aloud (*Read-Aloud Rhymes*, page 82), clarifying vocabulary as you read. Then read it aloud again, without stopping to clarify vocabulary.

Teacher Note

When reading poems aloud, always begin by reading the title and the name of the poet. Read poems slowly, allowing the students time to hear and imagine the words.

ELL Vocabulary

English Language Learners may benefit from discussing the following vocabulary:

stretch my hands: spread out my hands full length
curl my toes: bend or roll up my toes
yawn: open the mouth wide and breathe in deeply because of being sleepy

Read the poem aloud a third time, this time asking the students to pretend they are sleeping and then act out the poem as they listen

Teacher Note

If necessary, have the students spread out so they have room to move.

Kindergarten | 317

to it. Stop at the end of each action to have the students act out the poem with you. For example:

"I have to jump up
 out of bed
  [stop]
 and stretch my hands
  [stop]
 and rub my head,
  [stop]
 and curl my toes…"
  [stop]

After reading and acting out the poem, ask and briefly discuss:

Q *What are some things the poet does when she wakes up?*

Have a few volunteers share their ideas with the class.

Students might say:

"She jumps out of bed and stretches."

"She yawns."

"She shakes herself to wake up."

Point out that poets often use words in their poems that are fun to hear and act out. Explain that you will read two more poems with words that are fun to hear and act out. The students will listen with their eyes closed to imagine what's happening; then they will act the poem out as they hear it again.

3 Briefly Discuss Moving in a Responsible Way

Ask and briefly discuss:

Q *What will you do when you act out the poem to make sure you are moving in a responsible way?*

Students might say:

"I'll make sure I keep my hands to myself."

"I'll look around when I move."

"I'll stay in one place."

Tell the students that you will check in with them later to see how they did with moving in a responsible way.

FACILITATION TIP

During this unit, we encourage you to **avoid repeating or paraphrasing students' responses**. It is easy to habitually repeat what students say when they speak too softly, or to paraphrase them when they don't speak clearly. This teaches students to listen to you but not necessarily to one another. Try to refrain from repeating or paraphrasing and see what happens. Encourage the students to take responsibility by asking one another to speak up or by asking a question if they don't understand what a classmate has said. (See the front matter in volume 1 for special considerations for English Language Learners.)

Teacher Note

If the students have difficulty answering the question, suggest some ideas like those in the "Students might say" note; then ask, "What else will you do to move responsibly?"

Unit 5 ▸ Week 1 ▸ Day 1   **Exploring Words Through Poetry**

4 Read, Visualize, and Act Out "Shore"

Have the students close their eyes and make a picture in their minds as you read "Shore" by Mary Britton Miller aloud (*Read-Aloud Rhymes*, page 30). Read the poem twice, slowly and clearly, clarifying vocabulary on the first reading.

Suggested Vocabulary

shore: land along the sea, often covered with sand
damp: wet
seaweed: plants that grow in the sea

ELL Vocabulary

English Language Learners may benefit from discussing additional vocabulary, including:

gather: collect, pick up
shells: hard outer coverings of sea animals such as clams and snails
kneel: sit with your knees on the ground
wells: deep holes

Read the poem aloud a third time, this time stopping at the end of each action to have the students act out the poem with you. For example:

"Play on the seashore
 And gather up shells,
   [stop]
 Kneel in the damp sands
 Digging wells…"
   [stop]

After reading and acting out the poem, ask and briefly discuss:

Q *What does the poet say you can do at the shore?*

Have a few volunteers share their ideas with the class.

 **Note**

Acting out stories and poems is an effective way to build comprehension and vocabulary for students, particularly English Language Learners. Use this strategy whenever it seems appropriate to help the students understand text.

Students might say:

"You can play."

"You can pick up shells."

"You can look at the waves."

Kindergarten | 319

Exploring Words Through Poetry

Unit 5 ▶ Week 1 ▶ Day 1

**Note**

You may want to explain, or demonstrate, how to blow bubbles using soapy water and a wand.

▶ 5 Read, Visualize, and Act Out "Blowing Bubbles"

Follow this same procedure with the poem "Blowing Bubbles" by Margaret Hillert (*Read-Aloud Rhymes*, page 9). Have the students listen to it twice with their eyes closed and then act out the poem on the third reading. Clarify vocabulary during the first reading.

> **Suggested Vocabulary**
>
> **rainbow-colored:** having many different colors, like a rainbow
>
> **ELL Vocabulary**
>
> English Language Learners may benefit from discussing additional vocabulary, including:
>
> **dip:** put something into water and quickly pull it out again
> **gently:** carefully; not roughly
> **SPLAT!** wet popping sound

Ask and briefly discuss:

Q *What happens in this poem?*

> **Students might say:**
>
> "Someone blows a bubble."
>
> "The bubble gets big."
>
> "The bubble pops and goes 'SPLAT!'"

Explain that the students will hear and visualize more poems this week.

REFLECTING

Reflect on Moving Responsibly

Ask and briefly discuss:

Q *What was fun about acting out the poems today?*

Q *What did you do to move in a responsible way when you were acting out the poems?*

Being a Writer™

Q *Why is it important that we move responsibly when we act out poems?*

Without mentioning students' names, offer some observations about what went well as the students acted out the poems, as well as any problems you noticed. Encourage them to continue to think about how to move in the classroom in a responsible way.

FREE WRITING TIME

Write and Draw Freely

Give the students time to write and draw about anything they choose. Tell them that they might write a story or a poem. Remind them that they heard the poems "Wide Awake," "Shore," and "Blowing Bubbles" today and explain that they might write about a place they like to go or about something they like to do. Ask and briefly discuss:

Q *What might you write about today? Turn to your partner.*

Have a few volunteers share their ideas; then distribute paper and have the students write and draw freely.

EXTENSION

Read More Poems Throughout the Week

During this week's lessons, you will continue to read poems from *Read-Aloud Rhymes for the Very Young* with the students. In addition to these poems, you may wish to read aloud other selections from *Read-Aloud Rhymes* and encourage the students to act out or visualize the poems. Other short poems that lend themselves to acting out or visualization include "Whistling" (page 6), "Cat Kisses" (page 18), "Picnic Day" (page 32), "A Kite" (page 33), "Raindrops" (page 60), and "First Snow" (page 76).

Unit 5 ▶ Week 1

Day 2

Exploring Poems and Words

Materials
- "Toaster Time" and "The Frog on the Log" (*Read-Aloud Rhymes for the Very Young*, pages 50 and 21)
- Charted copy of "Toaster Time" (see "Do Ahead" on page 315)

In this lesson, the students:
- Hear, visualize, and discuss poems
- Explore interesting words in a poem
- Informally explore repetition
- Discuss and solve problems that arise in their work together
- Write and draw freely

GETTING READY TO READ

1 Gather and Briefly Review

Gather the class with partners sitting together, facing you. Review that yesterday they heard, visualized, and acted out poems. Tell the students that today they will hear and visualize more poems.

READING TIME

2 Read "Toaster Time" and Discuss Interesting Words

Teacher Note ▶

If necessary, explain that a toaster is a small machine that heats bread to make it crisp.

 **Note**

Consider showing a toaster and demonstrating how it works to toast a piece of bread. Alternatively, show and discuss the illustration on page 50 of *Read-Aloud Rhymes*.

Ask the students to close their eyes and make a picture in their minds as you read "Toaster Time" by Eve Merriam aloud twice, slowly and clearly (see *Read-Aloud Rhymes*, page 50).

Ask and briefly discuss:

Q *What is happening in this poem?*

Students might say:

"The toaster is going 'tick, tick, tick.'"

"She's making a sandwich."

"It goes 'POP!'"

322 | Being a Writer™

Unit 5 ▸ Week 1 ▸ Day 2

Exploring Words Through Poetry

Direct the students' attention to the charted copy of "Toaster Time." Explain that you will read the poem aloud again. Ask the students to think about words in the poem that they think are fun or interesting. Read the poem aloud slowly and clearly, pointing to each word as you read it. Ask:

Q *What words in the poem do you think are fun or interesting? Why?*

Students might say:

"I like 'tick, tick, tick.' That sounds like a toaster."

"'Tick' rhymes with 'quick.'"

"'Jamwich' is a funny word."

"I like 'POP!'"

Point out that the poet uses sound words that help us imagine hearing the toaster—*tick* and *pop*. Also explain that the poet makes up words to describe objects—*hamwich* and *jamwich*. Explain that all of these words help make the poem fun to hear.

◀ **Teacher Note**

If the students have difficulty identifying words they like, read the poem aloud again, point out a few words you like, and explain why you like them. Then ask the question again.

◀ **Teacher Note**

If necessary, direct the students' attention to the charted poem and discuss which words are real and which are made up.

3 Read and Visualize "The Frog on the Log"

Explain that you will read another poem with fun and interesting words in it. Have the students close their eyes and picture what's happening as you read "The Frog on the Log" by Ilo Orleans aloud twice, slowly and clearly (see *Read-Aloud Rhymes*, page 21).

> **ELL Vocabulary**
> English Language Learners may benefit from discussing additional vocabulary, including:
>
> **screech owl:** bird that eats small animals such as mice and frogs
> **in a flash:** very fast

Use "Think, Pair, Share" to have the students first think about and then discuss:

Q *What did you picture in your mind?* [pause] *Turn to your partner.*

Signal for the students' attention and have two or three volunteers share their visualizations with the class. As they share, reread the words from the poem that helped them make their mental pictures.

◀ **Teacher Note**

Listen as partners share their visualizations. If students are struggling, call for their attention and model visualizing by rereading the first two stanzas of the poem, closing your eyes, and thinking aloud about your mental picture and the words that helped you form it. If necessary, continue to model with stanzas 3 and 4 and stanzas 5 and 6.

Kindergarten | 323

Teacher Note

Repetition is a familiar poetic device that young writers can easily imitate. As the students write poems during the next two weeks, you might encourage them to repeat words in their poems. You might also wish to point out the rhyming words in "The Frog on the Log" (*frog/log, tree/scree, flash/splash*) and explain that poets sometimes use words in their poems that *rhyme* (sound alike).

Point out that the poet, Ilo Orleans, does something that many poets do—he repeats words such as *frog* and *log*. Explain that repeating words helps make the poem fun to read and hear. Reread the poem stanza by stanza and have the students repeat each stanza after you've read it.

Explain that tomorrow the students will have another chance to hear a poem, think about interesting words, and make a picture in their minds.

REFLECTING

4 Reflect on Sharing Ideas

Without mentioning students' names, offer some observations about what went well as partners shared their ideas today. Then invite the students to comment on what went well as they talked with their partner and what didn't go so well. Ask:

Q *What can you do next time [your partner doesn't want to share]?*

Q *Do you agree or disagree with [David's] solution? Why?*

FREE WRITING TIME

5 Write and Draw Freely

Explain that today the students may again write and draw freely about anything they choose. Remind them that they may wish to write and draw a poem. Direct their attention to the charted copy of "Toaster Time" and point out that poets sometimes write about everyday objects, such as the toaster in the poem. They also write about animals, as in the poem "The Frog on the Log."

Ask and briefly discuss:

 Q *What is something you could write about today? Turn to your partner.*

Have a few volunteers share their ideas; then distribute paper and have them write and draw freely.

EXTENSIONS

Discuss Rhyme in "Toaster Time" and "The Frog on the Log"

Tell the students that some poems rhyme, or use words that sound alike, while others do not. Explain that the poems "Toaster Time" and "The Frog on the Log" both have rhyming words. Show the chart of "Toaster Time" and read it aloud, asking the students to look and listen for words that rhyme.

Discuss Rhythm in "The Frog on the Log"

Invite the students to clap along with you as you read "The Frog on the Log" aloud. Emphasize the rhythm as you read (for example, "There *once* was a *green* little *frog*, frog, frog"). Then invite the students to chant the poem along with you, clapping on the stressed words.

Day 3

Unit 5 ▸ Week 1

Exploring Poems

Materials
- "Chums" (*Read-Aloud Rhymes for the Very Young*, page 40)
- Charted copy of "Toaster Time" from Day 2
- Charted copy of "Chums" (see "Do Ahead" on page 315)

In this lesson, the students:
- Hear, visualize, and discuss a poem
- Draw and write about their visualizations
- Share their partner's writing with the class

GETTING READY TO WRITE

1 Review and Discuss Poems

Gather the class with partners sitting together, facing you. Review that the students have heard and discussed several poems this week. Show the chart of "Toaster Time"; then ask and briefly discuss:

Q *How does a poem look different from a story?*

Q *What else do you know about poems?*

> **Students might say:**
> "Poems are short. Stories are long."
> "There are only a few words on the page."
> "They are like songs."
> "Some poems rhyme."

> **Teacher Note** ▶
> If the students have difficulty answering the questions, stimulate their thinking by suggesting ideas like those in the "Students might say" note. If students observe that poems rhyme, point out that some poems rhyme and some don't.

2 Read and Discuss "Chums"

Explain that today the students will hear another poem, make a picture in their minds, and draw what they imagine.

Show the chart of "Chums" by Arthur Guiterman. Ask the students to listen as you read the poem aloud twice, pointing to each word as you say it. Clarify vocabulary on the first reading.

Being a Writer™

Unit 5 ▶ Week 1 ▶ Day 3 Exploring Words Through Poetry

Suggested Vocabulary

chum: friend
begs: acts like he's asking for a treat
gives a paw: puts his paw in someone's hand as if to shake hands
finest: best

ELL Vocabulary

English Language Learners may benefit from discussing additional vocabulary, including:

paw: foot of a dog

Ask and briefly discuss:

Q *What did you find out about the poet's "chum," or friend?*

Students might say:

"He's a dog."

"He's the finest dog."

"He sits and begs."

"He can swim."

Ask the students to close their eyes and make a picture in their minds as you read the poem again. Then use "Think, Pair, Share" to have the students first think about and then discuss:

 Q *What did you picture in your mind?* [pause] *Turn to your partner.*

After partners have had a chance to talk, signal for their attention and have two or three volunteers share their visualizations with the class. As they share, reread the words from the poem that helped them make their mental pictures.

Think Before Writing

Tell the students that during writing time today they will each draw a picture of what they saw in their minds as they listened to the poem "Chums." Later they will share their pictures in pairs.

Kindergarten | 327

Teacher Note

Listen as the students share ideas. If they struggle to recall what they visualized, call for their attention. Have them close their eyes and visualize as you read the first stanza. Have a volunteer share his visualization and point out the words in the stanza that support his mental picture. Then repeat the process with the second stanza.

Give the students a few moments to think about what they will draw. Then have partners share their ideas.

Explain that the students might also add words to their drawing. Ask:

Q *What words might you add to your picture?*

Have a few volunteers share their ideas with the class. Tell the students that if they want to add words from the poem to their drawing, they can copy words from the chart. Encourage the students to use the ideas they shared with their partner and the class as they write and draw today.

WRITING TIME

4 Draw Visualizations

Ask the students to return to their seats, and have them draw what they pictured in their minds. As they work, walk around the room and observe them.

CLASS ASSESSMENT NOTE

Observe the students and ask yourself:

- Are the students able to draw their visualizations?
- Are their visualizations supported by the text of the poem?
- Are students adding words to their drawings?

If students are struggling, have them close their eyes and visualize again as you read the poem aloud.

Signal to let the students know when writing time is over. Ask them to look at their pictures and any words they have written and think about the following question:

Q *What words in the poem helped you draw your picture?*

Teacher Note

If necessary, reread the poem on the chart to help the students answer this question.

SHARING AND REFLECTING

 Share Drawings in Pairs and Reflect

Gather the class with partners sitting together, facing you. Have the students bring their drawings with them. Explain that today they will share their drawing and writing with their partner and then share with the class what their partner visualized and drew. Give the students a few moments to look at their drawing and writing; then have them share their drawings in pairs.

When most pairs have finished sharing, signal for their attention. Ask and briefly discuss:

Q *What part of the poem did your partner visualize and draw?*

Q *(Refer to the chart of "Chums.") What words from the poem did your partner use to help her draw her picture?*

Explain that next week the students will continue to explore poems together.

Week 2 Overview

UNIT 5: EXPLORING WORDS THROUGH POETRY

Read-Aloud Rhymes for the Very Young
selected by Jack Prelutsky, illustrated by Marc Brown
(Alfred A. Knopf, 1986)

Animals, bugs, and other topics are all presented in rhyme.

Writing Focus

- Students hear, visualize, and discuss poems.
- Students explore descriptive words in poems.
- Students generate lists of descriptive words.
- Students write shared and individual poems.

Social Focus

- Students listen respectfully to the thinking of others and share their own.
- Students build on one another's thinking.
- Students express interest in and appreciation for one another's writing.

DO AHEAD

- Preread this week's poems with your English Language Learners and show them related illustrations or photographs (such as a picture of a mouse), if possible.
- Prior to Day 1, select a familiar animal—such as a cat, dog, or rabbit—to be the subject of a shared poem. You might choose an animal the students have learned about or a class pet.
- Prior to Day 1, copy the poem "Mice" from *Read-Aloud Rhymes for the Very Young* (page 24) onto chart paper.
- Prior to Day 2, copy the poem "Fish" by Mary Ann Hoberman from *Read-Aloud Rhymes for the Very Young* (page 44) onto chart paper.
- Prior to Day 2, make sure you have lined writing paper available for the students to use during writing time. The students will use lined writing paper throughout this unit.
- Prior to Day 3, copy the poem "The Squirrel" from *Read-Aloud Rhymes for the Very Young* (page 58) onto chart paper.

TEACHER AS WRITER

"The poet doesn't invent. He listens."
— Jean Cocteau

This week, listen to the sounds of your classroom with a poet's ears. Jot down in your journal things you hear your students saying, as well as any other sounds you hear. Toward the end of the week, read over your notes and shape them into a poem. Keep in mind that your poem doesn't have to rhyme. Concentrate on using short lines and vivid language.

Unit 5 ▶ Week 2

Day 1

Exploring Poems and Words

Materials

- "Mice" (*Read-Aloud Rhymes for the Very Young*, page 24)
- Charted copy of "Mice" (see "Do Ahead" on page 331)
- Chart paper (both lined and unlined) and a marker

In this lesson, the students:

- Hear and discuss a poem
- Explore descriptive words in a poem
- Generate a list of descriptive words about animals
- Contribute to a shared poem about an animal
- Speak clearly and listen to one another
- Write and draw freely

GETTING READY TO WRITE

 Read "Mice" and Discuss Descriptive Words

Gather the class with partners sitting together, facing you. Review that last week the students heard, acted out, and visualized poems. Explain that this week partners will continue to talk about poems and share their ideas.

Ask the students to close their eyes and make a picture in their minds as you read "Mice" by Rose Fyleman aloud twice. Clarify vocabulary on the first reading.

> **Suggested Vocabulary**
>
> **nibble:** take small bites of

Ask and briefly discuss:

Q *What does the poet say about mice?*

Have a few volunteers share their ideas with the class.

332 | Being a Writer™

Students might say:

"They run around the house at night."

"Mice are nice."

"Mice have long tails."

Direct the students' attention to the charted copy of "Mice." Explain that you will read the poem aloud again. Ask the students to think about words in the poem that tell what mice look like. Point to each word as you reread the poem aloud. Ask:

Q *What words in the poem tell what mice look like? Turn to your partner.*

After a moment, signal for the students' attention and have a few volunteers share their ideas with the class. Label a sheet of chart paper "Animal Words" and write the word *mice* under the title. As the students report descriptive words for mice in the poem, record these on the chart (see the diagram on page 334).

◀ **Teacher Note**
Be ready to reread lines from the poem to help the students recall the words.

SHARED WRITING

2 Generate a List of Animal Words

Tell the students that you would like their help in adding animals, and words that tell what the animals look like, to the "Animal Words" chart. Ask:

Q *If you were going to write a poem about an animal, what animal would you write about?*

Have a few volunteers share their ideas. Record the names of a few animals they suggest on the "Animal Words" chart, leaving space between each one. Use "Think, Pair, Share" to have partners first think about and then discuss:

Q *What words might you use to tell what [a puppy] looks like? [pause] Turn to your partner.*

Exploring Words Through Poetry

Unit 5 ▶ Week 2 ▶ Day 1

Teacher Note

If necessary, stimulate the students' thinking by asking questions such as:

Q *What color is [a puppy]?*

Q *How big is it?*

Q *What is its [skin/fur] like?*

Q *What do its ears look like? Its nose? Eyes? Legs? Tail?*

Teacher Note

As you write descriptive words on the chart, point out that some words can be used to describe more than one animal. (For example, cats and mice can both have long tails and white teeth.)

Signal for the students' attention and have a few volunteers share their ideas with the class. As they share, record their ideas on the "Animal Words" chart.

Repeat this procedure to have the students generate descriptive words about other animals on the chart.

```
Animal Words

mice     long tail, pink ears, white teeth

snails   tiny, slimy, round shell

shark    gray, sharp teeth, striped like a tiger

kitten   pink tongue, sharp claws, purrs
```

Reread the words on the chart aloud.

3 Write a Shared Poem About an Animal

On a blank sheet of lined chart paper, model writing the title and the first line of a poem about one of the animals on the "Animal Words" chart. As you write, think aloud about what the animal looks like and include those details in the poem.

Teacher Note

You might say, "I want to write a poem about a snail. I will write *Snail* at the top of my page as the title. Then I'm going to tell about what a snail looks like by writing *Tiny, slimy,/In a round shell*." As you model writing, continue to look for opportunities to model approximating spelling and using the word wall.

Ask the students to close their eyes and imagine the animal you are writing about. Ask:

Q *What else could I add to tell what a [snail] looks like?*

Have a few volunteers share their thinking with the class.

Teacher Note

If the students struggle to think of words, stimulate their thinking by asking questions like those in the Teacher Note in Step 2.

Unit 5 ▸ Week 2 ▸ Day 1   Exploring Words Through Poetry

Students might say

"They are brown."

"They sometimes have stripes."

"It's shiny after they crawl by."

"They move real slow."

Use the students' descriptions to add a few more lines to the poem.

```
                    Snail

        Tiny, slimy,
        In a round shell.
        Brown and striped,
        It leaves a shiny trail behind.
```

Read the poem aloud, pointing to each word as you read it.

> **Teacher Note**
>
> You might say, "[Kenji] said that snails are brown, and [Glenn] said they sometimes have stripes. I will write, *Brown and striped*. [Kallie] said that it's shiny where they crawl by. I'll write *It leaves a shiny trail behind*."

REFLECTING

 Reflect on Writing Poems

Ask and briefly discuss:

Q *What was fun about writing our animal poem today?*

Explain that tomorrow the students will add to this poem and write an animal poem of their own.

> **FACILITATION TIP**
>
> Continue to try to **avoid repeating or paraphrasing students' responses**. Help them learn to participate responsibly in class discussions by encouraging them to ask one another to speak up or to ask a question if they don't understand what a classmate has said. (See the front matter in volume 1 for special considerations for English Language Learners.)

Kindergarten | 335

Exploring Words Through Poetry

Unit 5 ▸ Week 2 ▸ Day 1

FREE WRITING TIME

 Write and Draw Freely

Explain that today the students may write and draw freely about anything they choose. They might write about one of the animals on the "Animal Words" chart or about anything else they choose. Ask and briefly discuss:

 Q *What is something you could write about today? Turn to your partner.*

Have a few volunteers share their ideas; then distribute paper and have them write and draw freely.

Teacher Note

Save the "Animal Words" chart and the shared poem to add to on Day 2.

Unit 5 ▸ Week 2

Day 2

Exploring Words
Through Poetry

Writing Poems

In this lesson, the students:

- Hear and discuss a poem
- Explore movement words in a poem
- Add to a shared poem about an animal
- Write an individual poem about an animal
- Get ideas by listening to others

Materials

- "Fish" by Mary Ann Hoberman (*Read-Aloud Rhymes for the Very Young*, page 44)
- Charted copy of "Fish" (see "Do Ahead" on page 331)
- "Animal Words" chart from Day 1
- Shared poem from Day 1
- Lined writing paper for the students (see "Do Ahead" on page 331)

GETTING READY TO WRITE

 Read "Fish" Aloud

Gather the class with partners sitting together, facing you. Remind the students that yesterday they made a list of interesting words to describe how an animal looks. Explain that today they will hear a poem that describes how an animal moves.

Ask the students to close their eyes and make a picture in their minds as you read "Fish" by Mary Ann Hoberman aloud twice, slowly and clearly. Clarify vocabulary on the first reading.

> **Suggested Vocabulary**
>
> **flit:** move quickly and lightly
> **swerving:** changing directions quickly
>
> **ELL Vocabulary**
>
> English Language Learners may benefit from discussing additional vocabulary, including:
>
> **flying:** moving fast

Ask and briefly discuss:

Q *What is happening in this poem?*

Kindergarten | 337

Have a few volunteers share their ideas with the class.

> **Students might say:**
>
> "The fish are swimming really fast."
>
> "They are moving all over."
>
> "They are racing to get food."

Direct the students' attention to the charted copy of "Fish." Explain that you will read the poem aloud again. Ask the students to think about words in the poem that tell how the fish move. Point to each word as you reread the poem aloud. Ask:

 Q *What words in the poem tell how the fish move? Turn to your partner.*

After a moment, signal for the students' attention and have a few volunteers share their ideas with the class.

2 ▶ Add Movement Words to the "Animal Words" Chart

Direct the students' attention to the "Animal Words" chart and reread the names of the animals on it. Use "Think, Pair, Share" to have partners first think about and then discuss:

 Q *What words might you use to tell how a [snail] moves? [pause] Turn to your partner.*

Signal for the students' attention and have a few volunteers share their ideas with the class. As they share, record their ideas alongside the animal's name on the "Animal Words" chart.

Repeat this procedure to have the students generate movement words about other animals on the chart.

 **Note**

Support vocabulary development by having students act out the movement words they generate.

Teacher Note ▶

You might also have the students think about the sounds the animals make and add words that describe the sounds to the chart.

Animal Words

mice	long tail, pink ears, white teeth, running, hiding, nibbling
snails	tiny, slimy, round shell, slow, crawling
shark	gray, sharp teeth, striped like a tiger, swims fast, bites
kitten	pink tongue, sharp claws, purrs, scratches, zooms around the house

Reread the words on the chart aloud.

SHARED WRITING

3 Add to the Shared Poem from Day 1

Direct the students' attention to the shared poem from Day 1. Reread the poem, pointing to each word as you read it. Explain that you would like the students' help to add more to the poem. Ask:

Q *What can we add to our poem that would tell how a [snail] moves?*

Have a few volunteers share their thinking with the class. Use the students' suggestions to add details to the poem.

◀ **Teacher Note**

You might say, "[Ellen] said that snails crawl very slowly. I will write, *Crawl, crawl. Slow, slow.* I think I'll end the poem by writing, *Watch where you step!*"

Exploring Words Through Poetry

Unit 5 ▶ Week 2 ▶ Day 2

```
            Snail

   Tiny, slimy,
   In a round shell.
   Brown and striped,
   It leaves a shiny trail behind.
   Crawl, crawl.
   Slow, slow.
   Watch where you step!
```

Read the completed poem aloud, pointing to each word as you read it. Then read it again and have the students read along with you. Point out how the poem looks different from a story.

Explain that today the students will have a chance to write their own poems about any animal they choose.

4 Visualize and Generate Ideas for Animal Poems

Briefly review a few of the animal descriptions on the "Animal Words" chart; then ask:

Q *What animal will you write a poem about today? Turn to your partner.*

Ask the students to close their eyes and picture an animal as they listen to the following questions. Ask the questions one at a time, pausing after each to give the students time to think.

Q *What does your animal look like?*

Q *What does it sound like?*

Q *How does it move?*

Teacher Note

You might say, "Notice how I wrote our poem. It looks different from a story. The words of a story go all the way across the page in a long line, but the words of a poem are usually written in short lines with only a few words in each line."

Ask the students to open their eyes. Use "Think, Pair, Share" to have partners first think about and then discuss:

 Q *What words might you use in your poem to tell how your animal looks and moves?* [pause] *Turn to your partner.*

Signal for the students' attention and have a few volunteers share their ideas with the class. Encourage the students to use the ideas they shared with their partners as well as words from the "Animal Words" chart in their poems today.

WRITING TIME

 Write Animal Poems

Have the students return to their seats. Distribute lined writing paper and have them begin writing. Encourage them to look at the "Animal Words" chart to help them in their writing. Students who finish their poems may illustrate their poems or write more animal poems.

When the students have settled into their writing, walk around and observe.

CLASS ASSESSMENT NOTE

Observe the students and ask yourself:

- Are the students able to write about animals?
- Are the students able to think of words for their poems and write them?
- Do they use words that describe how animals look or move?

If you notice students having difficulty thinking of a first line after 5–10 minutes, signal for their attention and write some possible first lines on the board, such as *I think _____ are rather nice* and *I wish I had a _____*. Have the students each choose one line to begin with and continue writing their poems.

continues

> **CLASS ASSESSMENT NOTE** *continued*
>
> Students may or may not write pieces that look like actual poems. This is to be expected, as poetry is a challenging form to learn to write. At this point, accept all of their efforts to write about animals using descriptive words. If you have students who are eager to write poems about topics other than animals, allow them to do so.

Signal to let the students know when writing time is over.

SHARING AND REFLECTING

6 Share a Fun and Interesting Word and Reflect

Gather the class in a circle, with partners sitting together. Have the students bring their poems with them. Explain that each student will pick one fun and interesting word from his poem and read it aloud to the class. Give the students a few moments to choose their words; then go around the room and have each student read his word aloud, without comment.

When all of the students have shared, ask and briefly discuss:

Q *What word did you hear that got you interested in someone else's poem?*

Q *What did you hear that gave you ideas for a poem you might write?*

Ask the students to make sure their names are on their poems; then collect the poems. Tell them that they will write more animal poems tomorrow.

Teacher Note

Save the "Animal Words" chart to add to on Day 3.

Teacher Note

Save the students' poems to make into individual poetry books for each student before the Author's Chair sharing in Week 3. (See the Teacher Note on Week 3, Day 2, page 362.)

EXTENSION

Act Out Movement Words as a Game

Act out various movements and ask the students to guess what you are doing (for example, kicking, waving, turning, dropping, throwing, clapping, shivering). If you wish, include some unusual movements and encourage the students to make up words to describe them. You might also invite volunteers to act out the movements.

Unit 5 ▶ Week 2

Day 3

Writing Poems

Materials

- "The Squirrel" (*Read-Aloud Rhymes for the Very Young*, page 58)
- Charted copy of "The Squirrel" (see "Do Ahead" on page 331)
- "Animal Words" chart from Day 2
- Lined chart paper and a marker

In this lesson, the students:

- Hear and discuss a poem
- Add to the list of animal words
- Write shared and individual poems about animals
- Get ideas by listening to others

GETTING READY TO WRITE

 Read and Discuss "The Squirrel"

Gather the class with partners sitting together, facing you. Remind the students that yesterday they added movement words to the "Animal Words" chart and wrote poems about animals. Explain that today they will hear a poem called "The Squirrel." Ask:

Q *What do you think you know about squirrels?*

Ask the students to close their eyes and make a picture in their minds as you read "The Squirrel" aloud twice, slowly and clearly. Clarify vocabulary on the first reading.

> **Suggested Vocabulary**
>
> **whisky, frisky:** playful; full of energy
> **whirly, twirly:** turning quickly this way and that way
> **scampers:** runs quickly
> **broad:** wide
> **sail:** large sheet of cloth that makes a boat move when wind blows on it
>
>
>
> **ELL Vocabulary**
>
> English Language Learners may benefit from discussing additional vocabulary, including:
>
> **shell:** hard covering of a nut
> **snappity, crackity:** sound a shell makes when it is cracked open

344 | Being a Writer™

Unit 5 ▸ Week 2 ▸ Day 3

Exploring Words Through Poetry

Ask and briefly discuss:

Q *What is the squirrel doing in the poem?*

Students might say:

"He's climbing a tree."

"He's going down the tree."

"He's eating his supper."

Direct the students' attention to the charted copy of "The Squirrel." Explain that you will read the poem aloud again, and that you want them to look for words they think are fun or interesting as they follow along.

Read the first stanza of the poem aloud, pointing to each word as you read it. As a class, discuss:

Q *What words in this part of the poem do you think are fun or interesting? Why?*

Repeat the same procedure for stanzas two, three, and four.

Students might say:

"I like 'hippity hop.' That's how the squirrel runs."

"'Whirly twirly' is funny. He turns around."

"It says 'snappity, crackity.' That's how the shell sounds."

Add a few of the words the students identify to the "Animal Words" chart wherever they might be appropriate.

◀ **Teacher Note**

If the students have difficulty answering the question, stimulate their thinking by rereading lines from the poem.

SHARED WRITING

Write a Shared Poem About an Animal

On a blank sheet of lined chart paper, model writing the title and the first line of a poem about another animal from the "Animal Words" chart. As you write, think aloud about what the animal looks like and how it moves, and include those details in the poem.

Teacher Note

You might say, "I want to write a poem about a shark. I will write *Shark* at the top of my page as the title. Then I'm going to tell what the shark looks like by writing *Gray and smooth*." As you model writing, continue to look for opportunities to model approximating spelling and using the word wall.

Kindergarten | 345

Exploring Words Through Poetry

Unit 5 ▸ Week 2 ▸ Day 3

Ask the students to close their eyes and imagine the animal in your poem. Ask:

Q *What else could I add to the poem to tell what a [shark] looks like?*

Q *What could I add to the poem to tell how a [shark] moves?*

Have a few volunteers share their thinking with the class.

> **Students might say:**
> "Some sharks are striped like a tiger."
> "They have rows of big, sharp teeth."
> "Sharks are scary."
> "They swim around looking for food."

Use the students' suggestions to add details to the poem.

Shark

Gray and smooth.
Rows and rows of sharp teeth.
Striped like a tiger.
Looking for food.
Scary.

Read the completed poem aloud to the students, pointing to each word as you read it. Then read the poem again and have the students read along with you. Explain that today the students will have a chance to write a poem about another animal.

3 Visualize and Generate Ideas to Use in Animal Poems

Briefly review the "Animal Words" chart and then ask:

Q *What animal would you like to write a poem about today? Turn to your partner.*

Teacher Note

If the students struggle to think of words, stimulate their thinking by asking questions such as:

Q *What color is a [shark]?*

Q *How big is it?*

Q *What is its [skin/fur] like?*

Q *What do its teeth look like? Its nose? Eyes? Tail?*

Teacher Note ▸

You might say, "[Kim] said that sharks have rows of sharp teeth. I will write *Rows and rows of sharp teeth*. [Jacob] said that some sharks are striped like a tiger. I'll write *Striped like a tiger*. [Darrian] said sharks swim around looking for food. I will write *Looking for food*. I think I'll end the poem with *Scary*."

After a moment, have the students close their eyes and picture in their minds the animal they chose. Ask the questions that follow one at a time, pausing between each question to give the students time to think.

Q *What does your animal look like?*

Q *What does it sound like?*

Q *How does it move?*

Ask the students to open their eyes. Use "Think, Pair, Share" to have partners first think about and then discuss:

 Q *What words might you use in your poem to tell how your animal looks, sounds, and moves?* [pause] *Turn to your partner.*

Signal for the students' attention and have a few volunteers share their ideas with the class. Encourage the students to use the ideas they shared with their partners as well as words from the "Animal Words" chart in their poems today.

WRITING TIME

 Write Animal Poems

Have the students return to their seats. Distribute lined writing paper and have them begin writing. Students who finish their poems may illustrate their poems or write more animal poems. When the students have settled into their writing, begin to confer with individual students.

TEACHER CONFERENCE NOTE

During the next two weeks, confer with individual students by having each student tell you about his writing and read his writing aloud. Ask yourself:

- Is the student able to begin writing?
- Does he use descriptive words in his writing?

Accept and support the student's writing whether it resembles a poem or not. Other things you can do to support a student during the conference are:

- Ask the student to visualize and tell you about his topic.
- Ask questions to elicit more ideas.
- Have him read his writing aloud and think about where he might use movement or descriptive words.

Document your observations for each student using the "Conference Notes" record sheet (BLM1). Use the "Conference Notes" record sheets during conferences throughout this unit.

Signal to let the students know when writing time is over.

SHARING AND REFLECTING

 Share a Fun and Interesting Word and Reflect

Gather the class in a circle, with partners sitting together. Have the students bring their poems with them. Explain that, as they did yesterday, each student will pick one fun and interesting word from her poem and read it aloud to the class. Give the students a few moments to choose their words; then go around the room and have each student read her word aloud, without comment.

When all of the students have shared, ask and briefly discuss:

Q *What word did you hear that got you interested in someone else's poem?*

Q *What did you hear that gave you ideas for a poem you might write?*

Ask the students to make sure their names are on their poems; then collect the poems. Tell them that they will explore and write more poems next week.

EXTENSION

Illustrate Copies of the Shared Poems

Copy the shared animal poems from Days 2 and 3 onto regular-sized paper, leaving space on each paper for an illustration. Make copies of these for each student. Have the students illustrate the poems and then share their illustrations with the class.

Week 3 Overview

UNIT 5: EXPLORING WORDS THROUGH POETRY

Read-Aloud Rhymes for the Very Young
selected by Jack Prelutsky, illustrated by Marc Brown
(Alfred A. Knopf, 1986)

Animals, bugs, and other topics are all presented in rhyme.

Unit 5 ▶ Week 3 **Exploring Words Through Poetry**

Writing Focus

- Students hear, visualize, and discuss poems.
- Students explore descriptive words in poems.
- Students generate lists of descriptive words.
- Students write shared and individual poems.

Social Focus

- Students build on one another's thinking.
- Students listen respectfully to the thinking of others and share their own.
- Students express interest in and appreciation for one another's writing.

DO AHEAD

- Prior to Day 1, copy the poem "Crunch and Lick" from *Read-Aloud Rhymes for the Very Young* (page 67) onto chart paper.

TEACHER AS WRITER

"There are no new ideas. There are only new ways of making them felt."
— Audre Lorde

Select a classroom object or an object at home, such as a TV, refrigerator, or floor lamp. Study it. Think about its size, shape, features, and function. Then think of a person, animal, or thing the object reminds you of. Write a poem about the object. You might begin your poem with the line *A _____ is a _____* (for example, *A coffeepot is a trusted friend*).

Unit 5 ▶ Week 3

Day 1

Exploring Poems and Words

Materials

- "The Meal" and "Crunch and Lick" (*Read-Aloud Rhymes for the Very Young*, pages 68 and 67)
- Chart of "Crunch and Lick" (see "Do Ahead" on page 351)
- Chart paper (both lined and unlined) and a marker

In this lesson, the students:

- Hear and discuss poems
- Explore descriptive words
- Generate a list of descriptive words about foods
- Contribute to a shared poem about a food
- Speak clearly and listen to one another
- Write and draw freely

GETTING READY TO WRITE

 Read and Discuss "The Meal"

Gather the class with partners sitting together, facing you. Review that last week the students heard, visualized, and wrote poems about animals. Explain that today they will hear a poem called "The Meal," by Karla Kuskin, in which a man eats a very strange breakfast. Ask and briefly discuss:

Q *What do you usually eat for breakfast?*

Ask the students to close their eyes and make a picture in their minds as they listen. Read "The Meal" aloud twice, slowly and clearly. Clarify vocabulary during the first reading.

> **Suggested Vocabulary**
>
> **hastened to add:** said quickly
> **loveliest:** best; most delicious

Unit 5 ▶ Week 3 ▶ Day 1   **Exploring Words Through Poetry**

ELL Vocabulary

English Language Learners may benefit from discussing additional vocabulary, including:

turnip: kind of vegetable that grows underground

dessert: sweet food, such as cake or ice cream, that you eat at the end of a meal

Ask and briefly discuss:

Q *What does Timothy Tompkins eat for breakfast?*

Q *What's silly about this poem?*

Students might say:

"He drinks ketchup for breakfast."

"He doesn't eat cereal or regular stuff."

"He thinks his breakfast is delicious."

2 Read and Discuss "Crunch and Lick"

Ask the students to close their eyes and make a picture in their minds as you read another poem about eating. Read "Crunch and Lick" by Dorothy Aldis aloud twice, clarifying vocabulary during the first reading.

Suggested Vocabulary

trickle: drip slowly

Ask and briefly discuss:

Q *What foods does the poet say you can crunch?*

Q *What foods does she say you can lick?*

Direct the students' attention to the charted copy of "Crunch and Lick." Explain that you will reread part of the poem, and that you would like the students to listen for words that tell how a food

Kindergarten | 353

sounds or looks. Reread the first stanza of the poem aloud slowly and clearly, pointing to each word as you read it. Ask:

Q *What words did you hear that tell how a food sounds or looks? Turn to your partner.*

After a moment, signal for the students' attention and have a few volunteers share their ideas with the class. Reread the second stanza of the poem following the same procedure.

Point out that the poet uses interesting words to help us hear what popcorn, peanuts, and ice cream cones sound like when we eat them ("crunches," "crunching"). She also uses interesting words to help us see what popsicles look like ("rainbow-colored") and what chocolate sauce looks like when it drips down our chins ("it begins to leak and trickle").

SHARED WRITING

▶ 3 Generate Descriptive Words About Foods

Ask:

Q *If you were going to write a poem about a food, what food would you write about?*

Have a few volunteers share their ideas. Record their ideas on a sheet of chart paper entitled "Food Words," leaving space between each item on the list. Use "Think, Pair, Share" to have partners first think about and then discuss:

Q *What words might you use to tell what a [strawberry] looks like? [pause] Turn to your partner.*

Signal for the students' attention and have a few volunteers share their ideas with the class. As they share, record their ideas alongside the name of each food on the "Food Words" chart.

Teacher Note

If necessary, stimulate the students' thinking by asking questions such as:

Q *How big is a [strawberry]?*

Q *What is it shaped like?*

Q *What does it taste like?*

Q *How does it feel?*

Q *What sound does it make when you eat it?*

Unit 5 ▶ Week 3 ▶ Day 1

Exploring Words Through Poetry

Repeat this procedure to have the students generate descriptive words about other foods on the chart.

◀ **Teacher Note**

As you write descriptive words on the chart, point out that some of the words can be used to describe more than one food. (For example, both spaghetti and pizza can be stringy.)

```
                Food Words

   strawberry    juicy, heart shaped, sweet

   spaghetti     slurp, splat, messy, piled high

   pizza         cheesy, hot, stringy, delicious

   rice          sticky, tiny, puffy, fluffy
```

Reread the words on the chart aloud.

4 Write a Shared Poem About a Food

On a blank sheet of lined chart paper, model writing the title and the first line of a poem about one of the foods on the "Food Words" chart. As you write, think aloud about what the food looks, tastes, feels, and sounds like and include those details in the poem.

Ask the students to close their eyes and picture themselves eating the food you are writing about. Ask:

Q *What could I add to tell what a [strawberry] looks like?*

Q *What could I add to tell what it tastes or feels like?*

Q *What could I add to tell what it sounds like when you eat it?*

Have a few volunteers share their thinking with the class.

Teacher Note

You might say, "I want to write a poem about a strawberry. I will write *Strawberry* at the top of the page as the title. I'm going to start my poem with *Juice/ Running down my chin*. These words help us picture what it's like to eat a juicy strawberry." As you model writing, continue to look for opportunities to model approximating spelling and using the word wall.

◀ **Teacher Note**

If the students struggle to think of words, stimulate their thinking by asking questions like those in the Teacher Note in Step 3 (see page 354).

Kindergarten

Students might say:

"A strawberry is sweet."

"It is juicy."

"The seeds make little bumps on it."

Use the students' descriptions to add a few more lines to the poem.

> **Teacher Note**
>
> You might say, "[Brandi] said that strawberries are sweet. I'll add the word *sweetness* after *Juice*. [Austin] said they have seeds that make them bumpy. I'll add *Little seeds make bumps.*"

```
              Strawberry

          Juice, sweetness
          Running down my chin.
          Little seeds make bumps.
```

Read the poem aloud as a class, pointing to each word as you read it.

REFLECTING

5 ▶ Reflect on Writing Poems

Ask and briefly discuss:

Q *What was fun about writing our food poem today?*

Explain that tomorrow the students will add to the shared poem and write a food poem of their own.

FREE WRITING TIME

 Write and Draw Freely

Explain that today the students may write and draw freely about anything they choose. They might write a story or poem about one of the foods on the "Food Words" chart or about anything else. Ask and briefly discuss:

 Q *What is something you could write about today? Turn to your partner.*

Have a few volunteers share their ideas; then distribute writing/drawing paper and have them write and draw freely.

EXTENSION

Discuss Rhythm and Alliteration in "The Meal"

Invite the students to clap along as you read "The Meal" aloud. Emphasize the rhythm of the poem as you clap. Then invite the students to chant the poem after you, clapping on the stressed words.

You may also wish to point out that poets sometimes use words that start with the same sound (such as "Timothy Tompkins had turnips and tea/The turnips were tiny"), and that this makes poems fun to hear and say.

Teacher Note

Save the "Food Words" chart and the shared poem to add to on Day 2.

Unit 5 ▶ Week 3

Day 2

Writing Poems

Materials
- "Yellow Butter" (*Read-Aloud Rhymes for the Very Young*, page 67)
- "Food Words" chart from Day 1
- Shared poem from Day 1

In this lesson, the students:
- Hear and discuss a poem
- Explore color words in a poem
- Add to a shared poem about a food
- Write an individual poem about a food
- Get ideas by listening to others

GETTING READY TO WRITE

 1 Read and Discuss Color Words in "Yellow Butter"

Gather the class with partners sitting together, facing you. Remind the students that yesterday they made a list of descriptive words about foods. Explain that today they will hear another food poem and try writing their own.

Ask the students to close their eyes and imagine as you read today's poem. Read "Yellow Butter" by Mary Ann Hoberman aloud twice slowly and clearly, without showing the illustration. Clarify vocabulary during the first reading.

> **Suggested Vocabulary**
>
> **black bread:** bread made with dark rye flour
> **jelly:** fruit spread that does not have pieces of fruit in it
> **jam:** fruit spread with pieces of fruit in it

Explain that you will read the poem again. Ask the students to think as they listen about the color words the poet uses in the poem. Reread the poem aloud without showing the illustration. Then use "Think, Pair, Share" to have partners first think about and then discuss:

 Q *What color words did you hear?* [pause] *Turn to your partner.*

358 | Being a Writer™

Signal for the students' attention and have a few volunteers share their thinking with the class.

Point out that the poet uses color words to help the reader picture what the foods look like, and read a few examples from the poem ("yellow butter," "black bread"). Ask:

Q *What color words can we add to our "Food Words" chart?*

Write a few additional suggestions on the chart.

Food Words	
strawberry	juicy, heart shaped, sweet, red, green leaf on top
spaghetti	slurp, splat, messy, piled high, red sauce
pizza	cheesy, hot, stringy, delicious
rice	sticky, tiny, puffy, fluffy, white

SHARED WRITING

Add to the Shared Poem from Day 1

Direct the students' attention to the shared poem from Day 1. Reread the poem, pointing to each word as you read it. Explain that you would like the students' help to add more to the poem. Ask:

Q *What color words can we add to the poem to describe the [strawberry]?*

Q *What else can I add to the poem?*

Have a few volunteers share their thinking with the class.

Exploring Words Through Poetry

Unit 5 ▸ Week 3 ▸ Day 2

Students might say:

"You can say they have pink juice."

"Strawberries have a leafy, green hat."

"They are shaped like a heart."

Use the students' suggestions to add details to the poem.

> Strawberry
>
> Pink juice, sweetness
> Running down my chin.
> Little seeds make bumps.
> A leafy, green hat
> On top of a red heart.

Teacher Note ▸

You might say, "[Berta] said that strawberries have pink juice. I will add the word *Pink* to the first line of the poem. [Carl] said that strawberries have a green leaf on top that looks like a hat. I will add *A leafy, green hat*. I will end my poem by writing *On top of a red heart*."

Read the completed poem aloud, pointing to each word as you read it. Then read it aloud again and have the students read along with you. Explain that today the students will have a chance to write their own food poems.

▶ 3 Visualize and Generate Ideas for Food Poems

Briefly review a few of the food descriptions on the "Food Words" chart; then ask:

 Q *What food will you write a poem about today? Turn to your partner.*

After allowing time for partners to talk, ask the students to close their eyes and picture a food as they listen to the following questions. Ask the questions one at a time, pausing after each to give the students time to think.

Q *What does your food look like?*

Q *What does it feel like?*

360 | Being a Writer™

Q *What does it taste like?*

Q *What sound does it make when you eat it?*

Ask the students to open their eyes. Use "Think, Pair, Share" to have partners first think about and then discuss:

 Q *What words might you use in your poem to tell about the food you chose? [pause] Turn to your partner.*

Signal for the students' attention and have a few volunteers share their ideas with the class. Encourage the students to use the ideas they shared with their partners as well as words from the "Food Words" chart in their poems today.

WRITING TIME

4 Write Food Poems

Have the students return to their seats. Distribute lined writing paper and have them begin writing. Students who finish their poems may illustrate them or write more food poems.

When the students have settled into their writing, confer with individual students.

> **TEACHER CONFERENCE NOTE**
>
> Continue to confer with individual students by having each student tell you about her writing and read her writing aloud. Ask yourself:
>
> - Is the student able to begin writing?
> - Does she use descriptive words in her writing?
>
> *continues*

> **TEACHER CONFERENCE NOTE** *continued*
>
> Accept and support the student's writing whether it resembles a poem or not. Other things you can do to support a student during the conference are:
>
> - Ask the student to visualize and tell you about her topic.
> - Ask questions to elicit more ideas.
> - Have her read her writing aloud and think about where she might use sound, color, or other descriptive words.
>
> Document your observations for each student using the "Conference Notes" record sheet (BLM1).

Signal to let the students know when writing time is over.

SHARING AND REFLECTING

 5 Share a Fun and Interesting Word and Reflect

Gather the class in a circle, with partners sitting together. Have them bring their poems with them. Explain that each student will pick one fun and interesting word from his poem and read it aloud to the class. Give the students a few moments to choose their words; then go around the room and have each student read his word aloud, without comment.

When all of the students have shared, ask and briefly discuss:

Q *What word did you hear that got you interested in someone else's poem?*

Q *What did you hear that gave you ideas for a poem you might write?*

Collect the students' poems. Tell the students that tomorrow they will choose one of the poems they have written to share from the Author's Chair.

Teacher Note

Prior to Day 3, compile the students' poems into individual poetry books (including copies of the shared poems the class has written if you wish). You might leave the covers blank and allow the students to create titles and cover illustrations for their books.

Day 3

Unit 5 ▸ Week 3

Exploring Words Through Poetry

Author's Chair Sharing

In this lesson, the students:

- Reread their poems and choose one to share
- Share their poems from the Author's Chair
- Speak clearly and listen to one another
- Learn the prompt "I imagined" to express interest in one another's writing
- Write and draw freely

Materials

- Students' individual poetry books (see the Teacher Note on page 362)
- Self-stick note for each student
- Author's Chair

GETTING READY TO SHARE

1 Discuss Writing Poems

Gather the class with partners sitting together, facing you. Review that during the past few weeks the students have heard and talked about many poems and also written poems of their own. Ask:

Q *What was fun about writing poems?*

> **Students might say:**
>
> "We got to write about animals."
>
> "We used funny words like 'wiggle.'"
>
> "We got to act out the poems."

2 Choose a Poem for Author's Chair Sharing

Explain that you have gathered each student's poems into a book, and that you will hand back each student's poems in a moment. Explain that they will reread their poems, choose the one they like best to share with the class, and mark it with a self-stick note.

Distribute the students' poetry books and have them reread their poems and choose the one they would like to share. Have partners

Teacher Note

Support students who have difficulty choosing a poem by asking them questions such as:

Q *Which poem has words that you think are really fun or interesting?*

Q *Which poem is about something you really like?*

Kindergarten | 363

tell each other what poem they chose and why they chose it. Give each student a self-stick note to mark the poem they will share (model this, if necessary).

3 ▶ Teach the Prompt "I Imagined"

Write the prompt *I imagined* _____ where everyone can see it. Read it aloud, pointing to each word as you say it; then have the students read it aloud with you. Explain that you would like the students to make pictures in their minds as they listen to one another's poems today; then you would like them to use the prompt "I imagined" to describe what they thought about as they listened.

Ask and briefly discuss:

Q *Why is it important to speak in a loud, clear voice when you share your poem?*

Q *If you can't hear the person who is reading, how can you respectfully let him or her know?*

Q *What can you do to let the poet know you are listening to his or her poem?*

Encourage the students to be good listeners during sharing time.

SHARING TIME

4 ▶ Share Poems and Use the Prompt "I Imagined"

Call on a student to come to the Author's Chair and share her poem with the class. If necessary, remind her to read her poem's title and say her name as the author before reading the poem.

Take your seat in the audience and have the student share. At the end of the sharing, lead the audience in clapping. Use the prompt to comment on something you imagined as you listened; also mention

Teacher Note

You might say, "I imagined a snake slithering on the ground. The words 'hiss, hiss, hiss' made me imagine what the snake sounds like."

any interesting words in the poem that helped you create your mental image.

Invite the class to comment on the poem and allow the poet to call on two or three students who would like to comment. If necessary, prompt discussion by asking questions such as:

Q *What did you imagine as you listened to [Heather's] poem?*

Q *What interesting words did you hear in [Heather's] poem?*

Follow this same procedure to have other students share from the Author's Chair. If all of the students do not get to share today, assure them that there will be another opportunity for them to share their poems from the Author's Chair.

REFLECTING

5 Reflect on Sharing and Getting Ideas

Ask and briefly discuss:

Q *What did we do to be a respectful audience today?*

Q *What did you hear that gave you ideas for your own writing?*

Point out that writers can get ideas for their own writing by listening to other people's writing. Encourage the students to listen for things they might want to write about as they hear their classmates share their writing.

FREE WRITING TIME

6 Write and Draw Freely

Explain that today the students can write and draw freely about anything they choose. They might write a story or poem about one

---

Teacher Note

If there are students who do not get to share their poems today, plan another time so all of the students get to share their poems from the Author's Chair.

FACILITATION TIP

Reflect on your experience over the past three weeks with **avoiding repeating or paraphrasing students' responses**. Does this practice feel natural to you? Are you integrating it into class discussions throughout the school day? What effect is it having on the students? Are they participating more responsibly in class discussions? We encourage you to continue to try this practice and reflect on the students' responses as you facilitate class discussions in the future. (See the front matter in volume 1 for special considerations for English Language Learners.)

Teacher Note

This is the last week in this unit. Keep the current pairs together for Unit 6.

of the foods on the "Food Words" chart or about anything else. Ask and briefly discuss:

 Q *What is something you could write about today? Turn to your partner.*

Have a few volunteers share their ideas; then distribute writing/drawing paper and have the students write and draw freely.

Unit 6

Revisiting the Writing Community

Unit 6

Revisiting the Writing Community

During this final week of the *Being a Writer* program, the students reflect on what they enjoyed about writing this year, think about writing they might do during the summer, and each make a cover for a summer writing book. They reflect on how they built a caring community of writers and write a shared letter to next year's class about how to work well together. They also reflect on their relationships to others, build on one another's thinking, and express interest in and appreciation for one another's writing.

UNIT OVERVIEW

WEEK	DAY 1	DAY 2	DAY 3
1	**Reflecting on Writing** **Focus:** • Discussing what they liked about writing time • Writing about writing time • Sharing their writing from the Author's Chair	**Planning for Summer Writing** **Focus:** • Discussing what they might write about this summer • Illustrating the covers of their summer writing books • Sharing their illustrations	**Reflecting on Community** **Focus:** • Discussing how they worked well together this year • Writing a shared letter to next year's kindergartners about building a writing community

Week 1 Overview

UNIT 6: REVISITING THE WRITING COMMUNITY

Writing Focus

- Students write about what they liked about writing time this year.
- Students make covers for summer writing books.
- Students write a shared letter to next year's class about building the writing community.

Social Focus

- Students reflect on the writing community.
- Students reflect on their relationships to others.
- Students build on one another's thinking.
- Students express interest in and appreciation for one another's writing.

DO AHEAD

- Prior to Day 1, display a few books that the students have heard during the Being a Writer program this year. Also display any class books of student writing you have from the year.

- Prior to Day 2, make a class set of writing books by stapling together ten sheets of writing/drawing paper and a sheet of construction paper (for the cover) for each student. (You may want to use a second sheet of construction paper as the back cover for each book.) Write the title Summer Writing Book on each book. Leave space for the student's name and an illustration.

- Prior to Day 3, cut sheets of drawing paper into small squares (approximately 3" x 3") so each student will have one.

TEACHER AS WRITER

"Growth is exciting; growth is dynamic and alarming. Growth of the soul, growth of the mind."
— Vita Sackville-West

Reflect this week on your development as a writer and teacher of writing. What growth have you observed in yourself as a writer and writing teacher? Jot down your thoughts and feelings.

Unit 6 ▸ Week 1

Day 1

Reflecting on Writing

Materials
- Read-aloud books from earlier in the program (see "Do Ahead" on page 369)
- (Optional) Class books of student writing (see "Do Ahead" on page 369)
- Chart paper and a marker
- Author's Chair

In this lesson, the students:
- Discuss what they liked about writing time this year
- Write and draw about writing time
- Consider the impact of their behavior on others
- Reflect on how they benefit from the writing community
- Express interest in and appreciation for one another's writing

GETTING READY TO WRITE

1. Discuss Goals for the Week

Gather the class with partners sitting together, facing you. Explain that during this last week of the *Being a Writer* program the students will think about what they've enjoyed about writing and being a member of a writing community this year. Explain that they will also talk about writing they might do this summer.

Teacher Note

You will not assign new partners this week. Have the students work with their Unit 5 partner or with someone sitting near them.

2. Discuss What They Liked About Writing

Review that during writing time this year the students did many things that helped them become stronger writers. Direct their attention to the display of read-aloud books, and remind them that they heard many examples of good writing and learned what authors do to make their writing interesting and fun to read and hear. Read two or three of the titles aloud and briefly talk about each book.

Teacher Note

You might say, "We read *Mr. Santizo's Tasty Treats!* and found out that authors sometimes write true books with information about real people."

370 | Being a Writer™

Point to any class books you have displayed and remind the students that they wrote lots of stories, books, and poems this year. Read a few of the titles aloud. Review that they also worked with many different partners, helped one another by sharing ideas, and shared their writing with one another from the Author's Chair.

Use "Think, Pair, Share" to have partners first think about and then discuss:

 Q *What did you like best about writing time this year?* [pause] *Turn to your partner.*

When most pairs have finished talking, signal for the students' attention and have a few volunteers share their thinking with the class. Record a few of their ideas on a sheet of chart paper entitled "Things We Liked About Writing Time."

Things We Liked About Writing Time

- listening to stories
- writing about my dog
- talking with partners
- Author's Chair sharing

Explain that today the students will write and draw what they liked best about writing time. Later they will have a chance to share their writing from the Author's Chair. Ask:

 Q *What will you write and draw during writing time today? Turn to your partner.*

Encourage the students to use the ideas they shared with their partner in their writing today.

WRITING TIME

3 **Write and Draw About Writing Time**

Have the students return to their seats, and distribute writing/drawing paper. Have the students write and draw what they liked best about writing time this year. Encourage students who finish early to tell more by adding to their writing and drawing, or by writing about something else they liked about writing time on a new sheet of paper. As they work, walk around the room and observe.

> ### CLASS ASSESSMENT NOTE
>
> As you observe the students, ask yourself:
>
> - Are the students able to express their ideas through both writing and drawing?
> - Are the students writing with confidence and enthusiasm?
> - Does their writing make sense?
> - Do their illustrations relate to their writing?
> - Do they approximate spelling and use the word wall?
> - Do they tell more by adding to their writing or drawing?
>
> You might want to jot down notes about your observations to refer to when you begin planning your writing instruction for next year.

Signal to let the students know when writing time is over.

SHARING AND REFLECTING

4 **Reflect on How Others Might Feel**

Gather the class with partners sitting together, facing the Author's Chair. Have them bring their writing with them. Explain that some of them will share their writing and drawing from the Author's Chair. Ask and briefly discuss:

Q *What can we do to be a respectful audience when someone is sharing?*

Q *How do you think that will make the author feel?*

> **Students might say:**
> "We can listen."
> "We can tell the author what we liked about his writing."
> "It will make the author feel happy."

Write the prompts *I found out* _____ and *I want to know* _____ where everyone can see them, and remind the students to use these prompts when they comment on one another's writing.

5 Share from the Author's Chair

Call on a student to share his writing from the Author's Chair. Take your seat in the audience and have the student share. When the student has finished sharing, lead the audience in clapping; then wait quietly for students to comment. If students do not raise their hands to comment, raise your hand and comment about the author's writing. If necessary, ask the class:

Q *What did you find out by listening to [Jin's] writing?*

Q *What else would you like to know about [Jin's] writing or drawing?*

Allow the author to call on two or three students who would like to comment on his writing. Follow this same procedure to have more students share from the Author's Chair. If there is not enough time for all of the students to share, tell them the remaining students will share at another time.

◀ **Teacher Note**

If necessary, plan more sharing time so all of the students can share their writing from the Author's Chair.

6▶ Reflect on Author's Chair Sharing

Ask and briefly discuss:

Q *What do you like about sharing your writing with the writing community?*

Q *How does sharing your writing with the writing community help you become a stronger writer?*

Explain that tomorrow the students will think about writing they might do this summer.

Unit 6 ▸ Week 1

Revisiting the Writing Community

Planning for Summer Writing

In this lesson, the students:

- Plan for summer writing
- Make covers for their summer writing books
- Reflect on how they benefit from the writing community
- Get ideas by listening to others

Materials

- Class set of ten-page summer writing books (see "Do Ahead" on page 369)
- Markers, crayons, and other supplies for illustrating book covers

GETTING READY TO WRITE

1 Discuss Ideas for Summer Writing

Gather the class with partners sitting together, facing you. Review that yesterday the students wrote about what they liked about writing time this year. Remind them that they have written lots of stories, poems, and books this year.

Tell the students that one thing good writers do to become better writers is to write a lot. Explain that summer is a wonderful time to write because so many fun things happen during the summer. Use "Think, Pair, Share" to have partners first think about and then discuss:

 Q *What might you do for fun during the summer that you could write about?* [pause] *Turn to your partner.*

Signal for the students' attention and have a few volunteers share their thinking with the class.

2 Introduce the Summer Writing Books

Tell the students you will give them each a book to fill with writing and drawing this summer. Show one of the books you assembled, and point to and read the title (*Summer Writing Book*) aloud. Page

Teacher Note

If the students struggle to answer the question, stimulate their thinking by asking questions such as:

◂ **Q** *What fun places will you go to this summer that you might write about?*

Q *What will you do outside on a nice summer day?*

Q *What can you do during the summer that you can't do during the school year?*

Kindergarten | 375

through it, and explain that they can fill their books with poems, stories, or any other kind of writing they wish.

Explain that today the students will complete the covers of these books by writing their names and drawing pictures on them. Hold up one of the books and point to where the name and picture will go on each cover. Explain that when they are done, they will share their book covers with the class.

3 Think Before Drawing

Use "Think, Pair, Share" to have partners first think about and then discuss:

 Q *What picture might you draw on the cover of your summer writing book?* [pause] *Turn to your partner.*

Signal for the students' attention and have a few volunteers share their ideas with the class.

> **Students might say:**
>
> "I like to go swimming in the summer. I'll draw a picture of me swimming."
>
> "I'll draw me in my bedroom writing a story."
>
> "I'll draw me playing hide-and-seek in my yard with Kate and Ben."
>
> "I'll draw a picture of me helping my mom mow the yard."

Encourage the students to use the ideas they shared with their partner as they draw.

Teacher Note
If the students struggle to think of ideas, stimulate their thinking by suggesting some ideas like those in the "Students might say" note.

WRITING TIME

4 Illustrate the Summer Writing Book Covers

Have the students return to their seats and distribute the summer writing books. Remind the students where to write their names and draw their pictures on the covers.

As the students draw, circulate among them and encourage students to add labels or details to their pictures.

Signal to let the students know when writing time is over.

SHARING AND REFLECTING

 Share Book Covers and Reflect

Gather the class in a circle, with partners sitting together. Have them bring their book covers with them. Explain that each student will show and tell the class about her book cover. Give the students a few moments to think about what they will say; then go around the room and have each student share her book cover, without comment.

When all of the students have shared, ask and briefly discuss:

Q *What did you hear or see that gave you a new idea for summer writing?*

Q *Who else might be [riding a roller coaster] this summer?*

Q *How does sharing your ideas with the writing community help you become a stronger writer?*

Allow the students to take their books home.

EXTENSION

List Ideas for Summer Writing

Record some of the ideas the students generated in Step 1 of today's lesson on a chart entitled "Summer Writing Ideas." Have the students turn to the first page of their summer writing books and list some ideas they might write about this summer. Invite the students to use ideas from the chart to start their lists.

◀ **Teacher Note**

To further promote summer writing, you may want to collect the books and send them home with a letter explaining the purpose of the writing books and encouraging parents to create time for their child to write and draw during the summer.

Unit 6 ▶ Week 1

Day 3

Reflecting on Community

Materials
- Chart paper and a marker
- Small square of drawing paper for each student (see "Do Ahead" on page 369)
- (Optional) Hand mirror for each student

In this lesson, the students:
- Write a shared letter to next year's class about working well together
- Reflect on their contributions to the writing community

GETTING READY TO WRITE

 Introduce Writing About the Writing Community

Gather the class with partners sitting together, facing you. Remind the students that they have worked hard this year to build a writing community in which they are all friends who work well together and help one another. Explain that today they will write a letter together to next year's kindergarten class about how to work together during writing time. Explain that next year's kindergartners can read the letter and learn what they can do to build a caring writing community.

Making Meaning® Teacher
Some questions in this lesson are similar to those asked in the last week of the *Making Meaning* program. Read the lessons in both programs and decide if you want to teach them separately or combine them into one lesson.

WRITING TIME

 Write a Class Letter About Working Together

On a sheet of chart paper, write *Dear kindergartners, Here are some caring ways to work together during writing time.* Read the words aloud, pointing to each word as you read it. Use "Think, Pair, Share" to have the students first think about and then discuss:

Q *What advice would you give next year's kindergarten class about working together during writing time? What did we do this year that helped us work well together?* [pause] *Turn to your partner.*

Teacher Note
You may want to model a few ideas to stimulate the students' thinking and encourage them to phrase their ideas in a positive way. (You might say, "It is polite to look at people when they are talking. It is fun to share ideas with your partner.")

Unit 6 ▶ Week 1 ▶ Day 3

Revisiting the Writing Community

Signal for the students' attention; then have several volunteers share their thinking. As the students report their ideas, record them on the chart paper.

> **Students might say:**
>
> "Look at people when they talk. That shows you are listening."
>
> "Take turns talking. That way everyone gets a chance to talk."
>
> "During Author's Chair sharing, say something nice about the person's story."

If necessary, prompt the students' thinking with questions such as:

Q *What is important to do when you work with a partner?*

Q *What is important to do during sharing?*

Q *What did we do this year to be good listeners?*

Q *What is something that you know next year's kindergartners will enjoy during writing time?*

◀ **Teacher Note**

In Steps 4 and 5, the students draw self-portraits, which you will attach to the letter. Leave space below the writing for the self-portraits.

Dear kindergartners,

　　Here are some caring ways to work together during writing time:

- It is polite to listen quietly when your partner talks.
- It is fun to take turns sharing with your partner.
- It is helpful to talk so people can hear you.
- It is polite to look at your partner when he or she talks.
- It is nice to say what you like about someone's writing during Author's Chair sharing.

　　　　　　　　　　　　　　Sincerely,

　　　　　　　　　　　　　　Mr. Hansen's class

After the letter is written, read it aloud, pointing to each word as you read it.

Kindergarten

Revisiting the Writing Community

Unit 6 ▶ Week 1 ▶ Day 3

3 Model Drawing a Self-Portrait

Show one of the small squares of drawing paper. Explain that the students will write their names and draw *self-portraits*—pictures of themselves—on squares of paper like this one. Ask the students to watch as you model writing your first name at the bottom of the paper and drawing a picture of your head and shoulders. Explain that you are not drawing your whole body, since the paper is small.

Tell the students that you will paste their completed pictures on the letter so that next year's class will know who wrote it.

4 Discuss Details and Draw Self-Portraits

Have partners talk briefly about details they may want to include in their pictures, like eye or hair color, glasses, freckles, smiles, or curly hair. Then distribute the squares of paper and have the students return to their seats.

> **Teacher Note**
> Hand mirrors might be helpful to the students during this step.

Have the students write their names and draw their pictures on the squares of paper. As they work, circulate among them and encourage them to add details to their pictures.

SHARING AND REFLECTING

5 Share Self-Portraits and Attach Them to the Letter

Have the students gather and ask each student to share her self-portrait with the class. Attach each picture to the letter. Stop periodically to talk about where to place the next picture. After all of the pictures are attached, reread the letter with the class.

> **Teacher Note**
> As you attach the pictures to the letter, you might say something nice about each student's progress this year as a writer (for example, "[Tito] wrote some very imaginative stories about dinosaurs this year" or "[Amanda] is writing much longer stories now than she was at the beginning of the year").

6 Reflect on the Students' Growth as Caring Community Members

Share some observations about ways your students have grown as members of the writing community this year. (You might say, "I remember at the beginning of the year that some people didn't listen to their partner when they shared ideas. Now I see you looking at your partner and nodding. That shows me that you have learned how to listen respectfully to each other. I also remember that some people had trouble writing quietly at their table at the beginning of the year, but now I see people speaking in soft voices during writing time and raising their hand quietly when they have a question.") Ask:

Q *What else have you done to be a caring member of our writing community?*

Encourage the students to continue to write over the summer and to become caring members of their classroom writing community next year. Have the students take a moment to thank each other for their work together during writing time this year.

Appendices

Kindergarten Skill Development Chart

X = skill addressed

Skill/Convention:	Draw pictures to tell stories	Label pictures using letters or symbols that stand for writing	Approximate spelling using letter-sound correspondence	Write left-to-right and top-to-bottom	Use multiple letters to spell a word	Tell stories/ideas orally before writing	Use a word wall to spell high-frequency sight words	Use spaces between words	Write sentences	Capitalize the first letters of sentences	Use periods at the ends of sentences	Writing Process:	Prewriting	Drafting	Revision	Proofreading	Publication
K.1.1	X											K.1.1	X	X			X
K.1.2	X											K.1.2	X	X			X
K.1.3	X											K.1.3	X	X			X
K.1.4	X											K.1.4	X	X			X
K.2.1	X	X	X	X								K.2.1	X	X			X
K.2.2	X	X	X	X								K.2.2	X	X			X
K.2.3	X	X	X	X								K.2.3	X	X			X
K.2.4	X	X	X	X	X							K.2.4	X	X			X
K.2.5	X	X	X	X	X	X						K.2.5	X	X			X
K.2.6	X	X	X	X	X	X	X	X	X			K.2.6	X	X			X
K.2.7	X	X	X	X	X	X		X	X			K.2.7	X	X			X
K.2.8	X	X	X	X	X	X		X	X			K.2.8	X	X			X
K.2.9	X		X	X		X		X	X			K.2.9	X	X			X
K.2.10	X			X		X		X	X	X		K.2.10	X	X			X
K.3.1	X		X			X		X	X	X	X	K.3.1	X	X	X		X
K.3.2	X		X			X		X	X	X	X	K.3.2	X	X	X		X
K.3.3	X		X			X		X	X	X	X	K.3.3	X	X	X		X
K.3.4	X		X			X		X	X	X	X	K.3.4	X	X	X		X
K.4.1			X			X		X	X	X	X	K.4.1	X	X			X
K.4.2			X			X	X		X	X	X	K.4.2	X	X			X
K.4.3			X			X	X		X	X	X	K.4.3	X	X			X
K.5.1			X			X	X					K.5.1	X	X			X
K.5.2			X			X	X					K.5.2	X	X			X
K.5.3			X			X	X					K.5.3	X	X			X
K.6.1			X			X	X					K.6.1	X	X			X

384 | Being a Writer™

Bibliography

Ainsworth, Mary. "Patterns of Attachment Behaviour Shown by the Infant in Interaction with His Mother." *Merrill-Palmer Quarterly* 10 (1964): 51–58.

Anderson, Richard C., and P. David Pearson. "A Schema-Theoretic View of Basic Process in Reading Comprehension." In *Handbook of Reading Research* edited by P. David Pearson. New York: Longman, 1984.

Asher, James J. "Children Learning Another Language: A Developmental Hypothesis." *Child Development* 48 (1977): 1040–48.

———. "Children's First Language as a Model for Second Language Learning." *Modern Language Journal* 56 (1972): 133–39.

———. "The Strategy of Total Physical Response: An Application to Learning Russian." *International Review of Applied Linguistics* 3 (1965): 291–300.

Atwell, Nancie. *In the Middle: New Understandings About Writing, Reading, and Learning.* Portsmouth, NH: Heinemann-Boynton/Cook, 1998.

Battistich, Victor, Daniel Solomon, Dong-il Kim, Marilyn Watson, and Eric Schaps. "Schools as Communities, Poverty Levels of Student Populations, and Students' Attitudes, Motives, and Performance: A Multilevel Analysis." *American Educational Research Journal* 32, no. 3 (Fall 1995): 627–58.

Beck, Isabel L., Margaret G. McKeown, and Linda Kucan. *Bringing Words to Life: Robust Vocabulary Instruction.* New York: Guilford Press, 2002.

Bowlby, John. *Attachment and Loss.* Vol. 1, *Attachment.* New York: Basic Books, 1997.

Calkins, Lucy. *The Art of Teaching Writing.* Portsmouth, NH: Heinemann, 1994.

Contestable, Julie W., Shaila Regan, Susie Alldredge, Carol Westrich, and Laurel Robertson. *Number Power: A Cooperative Approach to Mathematics and Social Development Grades K–6.* Oakland, CA: Developmental Studies Center, 1999.

Culham, Ruth. *6+1 Traits of Writing: The Complete Guide for the Primary Grades.* Portland, OR: Northwest Regional Educational Laboratory, 2005.

———. *6+1 Traits of Writing: The Complete Guide, Grades 3 and Up.* Portland, OR: Northwest Regional Educational Laboratory, 2003.

Bibliography

Cummins, James. "The Role of Primary Language Development in Promoting Educational Success for Language Minority Students." In *Schooling and Language Minority Students: A Theoretical Framework*. Los Angeles: California State University, Evaluation, Dissemination, and Assessment Center, 1981.

Cunningham, Anne E., and Keith E. Stanovich. "What Reading Does for the Mind." *American Educator*, Spring/Summer 1998, 8–15.

Developmental Studies Center. *Blueprints for a Collaborative Classroom*. Oakland, CA: Developmental Studies Center, 1997.

———. *Ways We Want Our Class to Be*. Oakland, CA: Developmental Studies Center, 1996.

DeVries, Rheta, and Betty Zan. *Moral Classrooms, Moral Children*. New York: Teachers College Press, 1994.

Dewey, John. *Democracy and Education*. New York: Macmillan, 1916.

Fletcher, Ralph, and JoAnn Portalupi. *Writing Workshop: The Essential Guide*. Portsmouth, NH: Heinemann, 2001.

Flood, James, Dianne Lapp, and Julie M. Jensen. *The Handbook of Research on Teaching the English Language*. Mahwah, NJ: Lawrence Erlbaum Associates, 2002.

Freedman, Sarah W., Linda Flower, Glynda Hull, and J. R. Hayes. "Ten Years of Research: Achievements of the National Center for the Study of Writing and Literacy." In *A Handbook for Literacy Educators: Research on Teaching the Communicative and Visual Arts*, edited by J. Flood, S. B. Heath, and D. Lapp. Forthcoming.

Gambrell, Linda B., Lesley Mandel Morrow, Susan B. Neuman, and Michael Pressley, eds. *Best Practices in Literacy Instruction*. New York: Guilford Press, 1999.

Graves, Donald H. "Children Can Write Authentically If We Help Them." *Primary Voices K–6* 1, no. 1 (2003): 2–6.

Graves, Donald H. *Writing: Teachers and Children at Work*. Portsmouth, NH: Heinemann, 2003.

Hakuta, Kenji, Yuko Goto Butler, and Daria Witt. *How Long Does It Take English Learners to Attain Proficiency?* Santa Barbara, CA: University of California, Linguistic Minority Research Institute, 2000.

Harvey, Stephanie. *Nonfiction Matters: Reading, Writing, and Research in Grades 3–8*. York, ME: Stenhouse Publishers, 1998.

Herrell, Adrienne L. *Fifty Strategies for Teaching English Language Learners.* Upper Saddle River, NJ: Merrill, 2000.

Johnson, David W., Roger T. Johnson, and Edythe Johnson Holubec. *The New Circles of Learning: Cooperation in the Classroom.* Alexandria, VA: Association for Supervision and Curriculum Development, 1994.

Kagan, Spencer. *Cooperative Learning.* San Juan Capistrano, CA: Resources of Teachers, 1992.

Kamil, Michael L., Peter B. Mosenthal, P. David Pearson, and Rebecca Barr, eds. *Handbook of Reading Research, Volume III.* Mahwah, NJ: Lawrence Erlbaum Associates, 2000.

Kelley, Michael C. *Teachers' Reports of Writing Instruction at a High Performing Elementary School.* University of Delaware: Doctoral dissertation, 2002.

Kohlberg, Lawrence. *The Psychology of Moral Development.* New York: Harper and Row, 1984.

Kohn, Alfie. *Beyond Discipline: From Compliance to Community.* Alexandria, VA: Association for Supervision and Curriculum Development, 1996.

———. *Punished by Rewards: The Trouble with Gold Stars, Incentive Plans, A's, Praise, and Other Bribes.* New York: Houghton Mifflin Company, 1999.

Krashen, Stephen D. *Principles and Practice in Second Language Acquisition.* New York: Prentice-Hall, 1982.

———. *Second Language Acquisition and Second Language Learning.* New York: Pergamon Press, 1981.

———. "TPR: Still a Very Good Idea." *NovELTy* 5, no. 4 (1998).

———, and Tracy D. Terrell. *The Natural Approach: Language Acquisition in the Classroom.* Englewood Cliffs, NJ: Prentice Hall, 1983.

National Commission on Writing in America's Colleges and Schools. *The Neglected "R": The Need for a Writing Revolution.* New York: College Board, 2003.

National Council of Teachers of English. *What We Know About Writing: Early Literacy.* NCTE Writing Initiative. www.ncte.org/prog/writing/research/113328.htm.

National Governor's Association for Best Practices. *Making Writing Instruction Work.* Washington, DC: National Governor's Association Center for Best Practices, 2001.

Bibliography

Nucci, Larry P., ed. *Moral Development and Character Education: A Dialogue.* Berkeley, CA: McCutchan Publishing Corporation, 1989.

Optiz, Michael F., ed. *Literacy Instruction for Culturally and Linguistically Diverse Students.* Newark, DE: International Reading Association, 1998.

Piaget, Jean. *The Child's Conception of the World.* Trans. Joan and Andrew Tomlinson. Lanham, MD: Littlefield Adams, 1969.

———. *The Moral Judgment of the Child.* Trans. Marjorie Gabain. New York: The Free Press, 1965.

Ray, Katie Wood. *About the Authors: Writing Workshop with Our Youngest Writers.* Portsmouth, NH: Heinemann, 2004.

Resnick, Michael D., P. S. Bearman, R. W. Blum, K. E. Bauman, K. M. Harris, J. Jones, J. Tabor, et al. "Protecting Adolescents from Harm: Findings from the National Longitudinal Study on Adolescent Health." *Journal of the American Medical Association* 278 (1997): 823–32.

Schaps, Eric, Victor Battistich, and Dan Solomon. "Community in School a Key to Student Growth: Findings from the Child Development Project." In *Building School Success on Social and Emotional Learning*, edited by R. Weissberg, J. Zins, and H. Walbert. New York: Teachers College Press, 2004.

Schaps, Eric, Catherine Lewis, and Marilyn Watson. "Building Classroom Communities." *Thrust for Educational Leadership*, September 1997.

Schaps, Eric, Esther F. Schaeffer, and Sanford N. McDonnell. "What's Right and Wrong in Character Education Today." *Education Week*, September 12, 2001: 40–44.

Shefelbine, John, and Katherine K. Newman. *SIPPS: Systematic Instruction in Phoneme Awareness, Phonics, and Sight Words.* Oakland, CA: Developmental Studies Center, 2005.

Sulzby, Elizabeth. "Research Directions: Transitions from Emergent to Conventional Writing." *Language Arts* 69 (1992): 290–97.

Swain, M., and S. Lapkin. "Problems in Output and the Cognitive Processes They Generate: A Step Toward Second Language Learning." *Applied Linguistics* 16, no. 3 (1995): 371–91.

William, Joan A. "Classroom Conversations: Opportunities to Learn for ESL Students in Mainstream Classrooms." *The Reading Teacher* 54, no. 8 (2001): 750–57.

Blackline Master

On _____

Name: _____

Being a Writer — Reorder Information

Kindergarten

Complete Classroom Package — BW-CPK

Contents: Teacher's Manual (2 volumes) and 19 trade books.

Available separately

Teacher's Manual, vol. 1	BW-TMK-V1
Teacher's Manual, vol. 2	BW-TMK-V2
Trade book set (19 books)	BW-TBSK

Grade 1

Complete Classroom Package — BW-CP1

Contents: Teacher's Manual (2 volumes), Assessment Resource Book, and 21 trade books.

Available separately

Teacher's Manual, vol. 1	BW-TM1-V1
Teacher's Manual, vol. 2	BW-TM1-V2
Assessment Resource Book	BW-AB1
CD-ROM Grade 1 Reproducible Materials	BW-CDR1
Trade book set (21 books)	BW-TBS1

Grade 2

Complete Classroom Package — BW-CP2

Contents: Teacher's Manual (2 volumes), Skill Practice Teaching Guide, Assessment Resource Book, 25 Student Writing Handbooks, 25 Student Skill Practice Books, and 27 trade books.

Available separately

Teacher's Manual, vol. 1	BW-TM2-V1
Teacher's Manual, vol. 2	BW-TM2-V2
Skill Practice Teaching Guide	BW-STG2
Assessment Resource Book	BW-AB2
Student Writing Handbook pack (5 books)	BW-SB2-Q5
Student Skill Practice Book pack (5 books)	BW-SSB2-Q5
CD-ROM Grade 2 Reproducible Materials	BW-CDR2
Trade book set (27 books)	BW-TBS2

Grade 3

Complete Classroom Package — BW-CP3

Contents: Teacher's Manual (2 volumes), Skill Practice Teaching Guide, Assessment Resource Book, 25 Student Writing Handbooks, 25 Student Skill Practice Books, and 31 trade books.

Available separately

Teacher's Manual, vol. 1	BW-TM3-V1
Teacher's Manual, vol. 2	BW-TM3-V2
Skill Practice Teaching Guide	BW-STG3
Assessment Resource Book	BW-AB3
Student Writing Handbook pack (5 books)	BW-SB3-Q5
Student Skill Practice Book pack (5 books)	BW-SSB3-Q5
CD-ROM Grade 3 Reproducible Materials	BW-CDR3
Trade book set (31 books)	BW-TBS3

Grade 4

Complete Classroom Package — BW-CP4

Contents: Teacher's Manual (2 volumes), Skill Practice Teaching Guide, Assessment Resource Book, 30 Student Writing Handbooks, 30 Student Skill Practice Books, and 25 trade books.

Available separately

Teacher's Manual, vol. 1	BW-TM4-V1
Teacher's Manual, vol. 2	BW-TM4-V2
Skill Practice Teaching Guide	BW-STG4
Assessment Resource Book	BW-AB4
Student Writing Handbook pack (5 books)	BW-SB4-Q5
Student Skill Practice Book pack (5 books)	BW-SSB4-Q5
CD-ROM Grade 4 Reproducible Materials	BW-CDR4
Trade book set (25 books)	BW-TBS4

Grade 5

Complete Classroom Package — BW-CP5

Contents: Teacher's Manual (2 volumes), Skill Practice Teaching Guide, Assessment Resource Book, 30 Student Writing Handbooks, 30 Student Skill Practice Books, and 25 trade books.

Available separately

Teacher's Manual, vol. 1	BW-TM5-V1
Teacher's Manual, vol. 2	BW-TM5-V2
Skill Practice Teaching Guide	BW-STG5
Assessment Resource Book	BW-AB5
Student Writing Handbook pack (5 books)	BW-SB5-Q5
Student Skill Practice Book pack (5 books)	BW-SSB5-Q5
CD-ROM Grade 5 Reproducible Materials	BW-CDR5
Trade book set (25 books)	BW-TBS5

Ordering Information:

To order call 800.666.7270 * fax 510.842.0348 * log on to www.devstu.org * e-mail pubs@devstu.org

Or Mail Your Order to:

Developmental Studies Center * Publications Department * 2000 Embarcadero, Suite 305 * Oakland, CA 94606-5300